PUBLICATIONS OF THE TEXAS FOLKLORE SOCIETY

MODY C. BOATRIGHT, Editor
WILSON M. HUDSON, Associate Editor
ALLEN MAXWELL, Associate Editor

NUMBER XXVII

Mesquite and Willow

XXVII

PUBLISHED BY
SOUTHERN METHODIST UNIVERSITY PRESS
DALLAS

PUBLICATIONS OF THE TEXAS FOLKLORE SOCIETY.

MODY C. BOATRIGHT, Editor
WILSON M. HUDSON, Associate Editor
ALLEN MAXWELL, Associate Editor

NUMBER XXVII

Mesquite and Willow

XXVII

PUBLISHED BY
SOUTHERN METHODIST UNIVERSITY PRESS
DALLAS

Mesquite and Willow

Edited by

**MODY C. BOATRIGHT
WILSON M. HUDSON
ALLEN MAXWELL**

SOUTHERN METHODIST UNIVERSITY PRESS
DALLAS, TEXAS

LIBRARY OF CONGRESS CATALOG CARD NUMBER: 56-12566

PRINTED IN THE UNITED STATES OF AMERICA

BY WILKINSON PRINTING COMPANY: DALLAS, TEXAS

Preface

THE TITLE OF THIS BOOK alludes to two branches of folklore that exist side by side in Texas, the English and the Mexican. The English tradition is symbolized by the willow and the Mexican by the mesquite. *Mezquite* is the Spaniards' approximation of Nahuatl *mizquitl,* and of course Mexican folklore contains a mixture of Spanish and Indian elements.

The mesquite and the willow both grow in Texas; the two may be found in the same place, but the mesquite has a much wider range because it can live in dry country. Mesquite belongs mainly to that part of Texas where the Mexican influence was the strongest, the country below San Antonio once occupied by Spanish and Mexican ranchers who traced their land titles back to grants made by the king of Spain. Their cattle and horses liked the shade of the mesquite and its sweet beans that would carry them through times of drouth when the grass failed, and the vaqueros knew that a few leaves of the mesquite placed in a hat would keep them from getting sunstroke.

In the symbolic sense, Mr. Paredes' contribution is mesquite and Mr. McNeil's is willow. Mr. Hendren's retelling of a Mexican folktale in English ballad stanzas grafts willow onto mesquite stock. Among the people, the Mexican and English traditions have remained separate and distinct. In this book there is more mesquite than willow, and a few articles lie outside the symbolism of the two trees.

v

Stith Thompson, editor of the first publication of the Texas Folklore Society in 1916 and now a foremost folklore scholar, gave the principal address at the Society's fortieth meeting in 1956. We are very happy to have his address in this volume.

Mody C. Boatright
Wilson M. Hudson
Allen Maxwell

Austin and Dallas
March 5, 1957

Contents

Mesquite and Willow

The Legend of Gregorio Cortez

AMÉRICO PAREDES

THAT WAS GOOD SINGING, and a good song; give the man a drink. Not like these *pachucos* nowadays, mumbling damn-foolishness into a microphone; it is not done that way. Men should sing with their heads thrown back, with their mouths wide open and their eyes shut. Fill your lungs, so they can hear you at the pasture's farther end. And when you sing, sing songs like "El Corrido de Gregorio Cortez." There's a song that makes the hackles rise. You can almost see him there—Gregorio Cortez, with his pistol in his hand.

He was a man, a Border man. What did he look like? Well, that is hard to tell. Some say he was short and some say he was tall; some say he was Indian brown and some say he was blond like a newborn cockroach. But I'd say he was not too dark and not too fair, not too thin and not too fat, not too short and not too tall; and he looked just a little bit like me. But does it matter so much what he looked like? He was a man, very much of a man; and he was a Border man. Some say he was born in Matamoros; some say Reynosa; some say Hidalgo County on the other side. And I guess others will say other things. But Matamoros or Reynosa or Hidalgo, it's all the same Border; and short or tall, dark or fair, it's the man that counts. And that's what he was, a man.

Not a gunman, no, not a bravo. He never came out of a cantina wanting to drink up the sea at one gulp. Not that kind

3

of man, if you can call that kind a man. No, that wasn't Gregorio
Cortez at all. He was a peaceful man, a hard-working man like
you and me. He could shoot. Forty-four and thirty-thirty, they
were the same to him. He could put five bullets into a piece of
board and not make but one hole, and quicker than you could
draw a good deep breath. Yes, he could shoot. But he could
also work.

He was a vaquero, and a better one there has not ever been,
from Laredo to the mouth. He could talk to horses, and they
would understand. They would follòw him around, like dogs,
and no man knew a good horse better than Gregorio Cortez.
As for cattle, he could set up school for your best *caporal.* And
if an animal was lost, and nobody could pick up a trail, they
would send for Gregorio Cortez. He could always find a trail.
There was no better tracker in all the Border country, nor a
man who could hide his tracks better if he wanted to. That was
Gregorio Cortez, the best vaquero and range man that there
ever was.

But that is not all. You farmers, do you think that Gregorio
Cortez did not know your business too? You could have told
him nothing about cotton or beans or corn. He knew it all. He
could look into the sky of a morning and smell it, sniff it the
way a dog sniffs, and tell you what kind of weather there was
going to be. And he would take a piece of dirt in his hands and
rub it back and forth between his fingers—to see if the land had
reached its point—and you would say he was looking into it.
And perhaps he was, for Gregorio Cortez was the seventh son
of a seventh son.

You piddling modern farmers, vain of yourselves when you
make a bale: you should have seen the crops raised by Gregorio
Cortez. And when harvesting came, he was in there with the
rest. Was it shucking corn? All you could see was the shucks
fly and the pile grow, until you didn't know there was a man
behind the pile. But he was even better at cotton-picking time.
He would bend down and never raise his head till he came out

the other end, and he would be halfway through another row before the next man was through with his. And don't think the row he went through wasn't clean. No flags, no streamers, nothing left behind, nothing but clean, empty burrs where he had passed. It was the same when clearing land. There were men who went ahead of him, cutting fast along their strip in the early morning, but by noontime the man ahead was always Gregorio Cortez, working at his own pace, talking little and not singing very much, and never acting up.

For Gregorio Cortez was not of your noisy, hell-raising type. That was not his way. He always spoke low, and he was always polite, whomever he was speaking to. And when he spoke to men older than himself he took off his hat and held it over his heart. A man who never raised his voice to parent or elder brother, and never disobeyed; that was Gregorio Cortez, and that was the way men were in this country along the river. That was the way they were before these modern times came, and God went away.

He should have stayed on the Border; he should not have gone up above, into the North. But it was going to be that way, and that was the way it was. Each man has a certain lot in life, and no other thing but that will be his share. People were always coming down from places in the North, from Dallas and San Antonio and Corpus and Fort Worth. And they would say, "Gregorio Cortez, why don't you go north? There is much money to be made. Stop eating beans and tortillas and that rubbery jerked beef. One of these days you're going to put out one of your eyes, pull and pull with your teeth on that stuff and it suddenly lets go. It's a wonder all you Border people are not one-eyed. Come up above with us, where you can eat white bread and ham."

But Gregorio Cortez would only smile, because he was a peaceful man and did not take offense. He did not like white bread and ham; it made people flatulent and dull. And he liked it where he was. So he always said, "I will stay here."

But Gregorio Cortez had a brother, a younger brother named Román. Now Román was just like the young men of today, loud-mouthed and discontented. He was never happy where he was, and to make it worse he loved a joke more than any other thing. He would think nothing of playing a joke on a person twice his age. He had no respect for anyone, and that is why he ended like he did. But that is yet to tell.

Román talked to Gregorio and begged him that they should move away from the river and go up above, where there was much money to be made. And he talked and begged so that finally Gregorio Cortez said he would go with his brother Román, and they saddled their horses and rode away to the North.

Well, they did not grow rich, though things went well with them because they were good workers. Sometimes they picked cotton; sometimes they were vaqueros, and sometimes they cleared land for the Germans. Finally they came to a place called El Carmen, and there they settled down and farmed. And that was how Gregorio Cortez came to be in the County of El Carmen, where the tragedy took place.

Román owned two horses, two beautiful sorrels that were just alike, the same color, the same markings, and the same size. You could not have told them apart, except that one of them was lame. There was an American who owned a little sorrel mare. This man was dying to get Román's sorrel—the good one —and every time they met he would offer to swap the mare for the horse. But Román did not think much of the mare. He did not like it when the American kept on trying to make him trade.

"I wonder what this Gringo thinks," Román said to himself. "He takes me for a fool. But I'm going to make him such a trade that he will remember me forever."

And Román laughed a big-mouthed laugh. He thought it would be a fine joke, besides being a good trade. There were mornings when the American went to town in his buggy along a narrow road. So Román saddled the lame sorrel, led him a little way along the road, and stopped under a big mesquite that bordered on the fence. He fixed it so the spavined side was against the mesquite. Román waited a little while, and soon he heard the buggy coming along the road. Then he got in the saddle and began picking mesquites off the tree and eating them. When the American came around the bend, there was Román on his sorrel horse. The American stopped his buggy abreast of Román and looked at the horse with much admiration. It was a fine animal, exactly like the other one, but the American could not see the spavined leg.

"Changed your mind?" the American said.

Román stopped chewing on a mesquite and said, "Changed my mind about what?"

"About trading that horse for my mare."

"You're dead set on trading your mare for this horse of mine?" Román said.

"You know I am," the American said. "Are you ready to come round?"

"I'm in a trading mood," said Román. "With just a little arguing you might convince me to trade this horse for that worthless mare of yours. But I don't know; you might go back on the deal later on."

"I never go back on my word," the American said. "What do you think I am, a Mexican?"

"We'll see, we'll see," Román said. "How much are you willing to give in hand?"

"Enough to give you the first square meal you've had in your life," the American said.

Román laughed, and it was all he could do to keep from guffawing. He knew who was getting the best of things.

So they made the deal, with Román still sitting on his spavined horse under the tree, chewing on mesquites.

"Where's the mare?" Román said.

"She's in my yard," said the American, "hung to a tree. You

go get her and leave the horse there for me because I'm in a
hurry to get to town."

That was how Román had figured it, so he said, "All right,
I'll do it, but when I finish with these mesquites."

"Be sure you do, then," the American said.

"Sure, sure," said Román. "No hurry about it, is there?"

"All right," the American said, "take your time." And he
drove off leaving Román still sitting on his horse under the
mesquite, and as he drove off the American said, "Now isn't
that just like a Mexican. He takes his time."

Román waited until the American was gone, and then he
stopped eating mesquites. He got off and led the horse down
the road to the American's yard and left him there in place of
the little sorrel mare. On the way home Román almost fell off
his saddle a couple of times, laughing and laughing to think of
the face the American would pull when he got home that night.

The next morning, when Gregorio Cortez got up he said to
his brother Román, "Something is going to happen today."

"Why do you say that?" Román asked him.

"I don't know," said Gregorio Cortez. "I just know that
something is going to happen today. I feel it. Last night my
wife began to sigh for no reason at all. She kept sighing and
sighing half the night, and she didn't know why. Her heart was
telling her something, and I know some unlucky thing will
happen to us today."

But Román just laughed, and Gregorio went inside the
house to shave. Román followed him into the house and stood
at the door while Gregorio shaved. It was a door made in two
sections; the upper part was open and Román was leaning on
the lower part, like a man leaning out of a window or over a
fence. Román began to tell Gregorio about the horse trade he
had made the day before, and he laughed pretty loud about it,
because he thought it was a good joke. Gregorio Cortez just
shaved, and he didn't say anything.

When what should pull in at the gate but a buggy, and the

American got down, and the Major Sheriff of the County of El Carmen got down too. They came into the yard and up to where Román was leaning over the door, looking out.

The American had a very serious face. "I came for the mare you stole yesterday morning," he said.

Román laughed a big-mouthed laugh. "What did I tell you, Gregorio?" he said. "This Gringo sanavabiche has backed down on me."

Now there are three saints that the Americans are especially fond of—Santa Anna, San Jacinto, and Sanavabiche—and of the three it is Sanavabiche that they pray to most. Just listen to an American at any time of day. You may not understand anything else he says, but you are sure to hear him say, "Sanavabiche! Sanavabiche! Sanavabiche!" Every hour of the day. But they'll get very angry if you say it too, perhaps because it is a saint that belongs to them alone.

And so it was with the Major Sheriff of the County of El Carmen. Just as the words "Gringo sanavabiche" came out of Román's mouth, the sheriff whipped out his gun and shot Román. He shot Román as he stood there with his head thrown back, laughing at his joke. The sheriff shot him in the face, right in the open mouth, and Román fell away from the door, at the Major Sheriff's feet.

And then Gregorio Cortez stood at the door, where his brother had stood, with his pistol in his hand. Now he and the Major Sheriff met, each one pistol in hand, as men should meet when they fight for what is right. For it is a pretty thing to see, when two men stand up for their right, with their pistols in their hands, front to front and without fear. And so it was, for the Major Sheriff also was a man.

Yes, the Major Sheriff was a man; he was a game cock that had won in many pits, but in Gregorio Cortez he met a cockerel that pecked his comb. The Major Sheriff shot first, and he missed; and Gregorio Cortez shot next, and he didn't miss. Three times did they shoot, three times did the Major Sheriff miss, and three times did Gregorio Cortez shoot the sheriff of El Carmen. The Major Sheriff fell dead at the feet of Gregorio Cortez, and it was in this way that Gregorio Cortez killed the first sheriff of many that he was to kill.

When the Major Sheriff fell, Gregorio Cortez looked up, and the other American said, "Don't kill me; I am unarmed."

"I will not kill you," said Gregorio Cortez. "But you'd better go away."

So the American went away. He ran into the brush and kept on running until he came to town and told all the other sheriffs that the Major Sheriff was dead.

Meanwhile Gregorio Cortez knew that he too must go away. He was not afraid of the law; he knew the law, and he knew that he had the right. But if he stayed the Rangers would come, and the Rangers have no regard for law. You know what kind of men they are. When the Governor of the State wants a new Ranger he asks his sheriffs, "Bring all the criminals to me." And from the murderers he chooses a Ranger, because no one can be a Ranger who has not killed a man. So Gregorio Cortez knew that the best thing for him was to go away, and his first thought was of the Border, where he had been born. He went in the house and got his thirty-thirty, and then he looked around for the best horse he had. It is a long way from El Carmen to the Border, all of 500 miles. The first thing he saw in the corral was the little sorrel mare. Gregorio Cortez took a good look at her, and he knew she was no ordinary mare.

"You're worth a dozen horses," said Gregorio Cortez, and he saddled the little mare.

But by then the whole wasp's nest was beginning to buzz. The President of the United States offered a thousand dollars for him, and many men went out to get Gregorio Cortez. The Major Sheriffs of the counties and all of their sheriffs were out. There were Rangers from the counties too, all armed to the teeth, and the King Ranch Rangers from the Capital, the meanest of them all. Every road was blocked and every bridge guarded. There were trackers out with those dogs they call hounds, that can follow a track better than the best tracker. They had railroad cars loaded with guns and ammunition, chasing him. The women and children stayed in the houses behind locked doors, such was the fear they all had of Gregorio Cortez. Every town from the Capital to the Border was watching out for him. The brush and the fields were full of men, trying to pick up his trail. And Gregorio Cortez rode out for the Border, through brush and fields and barbed wire fences, on his little sorrel mare.

He rode and rode until he came to a great broad plain, and he started to ride across. But just as he did one of the sheriffs saw him. The sheriff saw him, but he hid behind a bush because he was afraid to take him on alone. So he called the other sheriffs together and they went off after Gregorio Cortez just as he came out upon the plain. There were three hundred of them.

Away went the mare, as if she had been shot from a gun, and behind her came the sheriffs, shooting and riding hard. And so they rode across the wide plain, until one by one their horses foundered and fell to the ground and died. But still the little mare ran on, as fresh as a lettuce leaf, and pretty soon she was running all alone.

"They'll never catch me like that," said Gregorio Cortez, "not even with those dogs called hounds."

Another big bunch of sheriffs rode up, and they chased him to the edge of the plain, and into the brush went Cortez, with the trackers after him, but they did not chase him long. One moment there was a trail to follow, and next moment there was none. And the dogs called hounds sat down and howled, and the men scratched their heads and went about in circles looking for the trail. And Gregorio Cortez went on, leaving no trail, so that people thought he was riding through the air.

There were armed men everywhere, and he could not stop to eat or drink, because wherever he tried to stop armed men

were there before him. So he had to ride on and on. Now they
saw him, now they lost him, and so the chase went on. Many
more horses foundered, but the mare still ran, and Gregorio
Cortez rode on and on, pursued by hundreds and fighting
hundreds every place he went.

"So many mounted Rangers," said Gregorio Cortez, "to
catch just one Mexican."

It was from the big bunches that he ran. Now and again
he would run into little ones of ten or a dozen men, and they
were so scared of him that they would let him pass. Then,
when he was out of range they would shoot at him, and he
would shoot back at them once or twice, so they could go back
and say, "We met up with Gregorio Cortez, and we traded shots
with him." But from the big ones he had to run. And it was the
little sorrel mare that took him safe away, over the open spaces
and into the brush, and once in the brush, they might as well
have been following a star.

So it went for a day, and when night fell Cortez arrived at
a place called Los Fresnos and called at a Mexican house.
When the man came out, Cortez told him, "I am Gregorio
Cortez."

That was all he had to say. He ate and drank, and the man
of the house offered Gregorio Cortez his own horse, and his
rifle and his saddle. But Cortez only thanked the man; he would
not give up his little sorrel mare.

Cortez was sitting there, drinking a cup of coffee, when the
Major Sheriff of Los Fresnos came up with his three hundred
men. All the other people ran out of the house and hid, and
no one was left inside, only Gregorio Cortez with his pistol
in his hand.

Then the Major Sheriff called out, in a weepy voice, as the
corrido says. He sounded as if he wanted cry, but it was all
done to deceive Gregorio Cortez.

"Cortez," the Major Sheriff said, "hand over your weapons.
I did not come to kill you. I am your friend."

"If you come as my friend," said Gregorio Cortez, "why did you bring three hundred men? Why have you made me a corral?"

The Major Sheriff knew that he had been caught in a lie, and the fighting began. Cortez killed the Major Sheriff and the second sheriff under him, and he killed many sheriffs more. Some of the sheriffs got weak in the knees, and many ran away.

"Don't go away," said Gregorio Cortez. "I am the man you are looking for. I am Gregorio Cortez."

They were more than three hundred, but he jumped their corral, and he rode away again, and those three hundred did not chase him any more.

He rode on and on until he came to a river called the San Antonio. It was not much of a river but the banks were steep and high, and he could not find a ford. So he rode to a ranch house near by where they were holding a *baile* because the youngest child of the house had been baptized that day, and he asked the man of the house about a ford.

"There are only two fords," the man said. "One is seven miles up river and the other is seven miles down."

"I will take another look at the river," said Gregorio Cortez.

He left the *baile* and rode slowly to the river. Far below he could see the water flowing; he could barely see it because it was so dark. He stood there thinking, trying to figure out a way, when he heard the music at the *baile* stop.

He knew the Rangers were at the *baile* now, so he leaned over in his saddle and whispered in the mare's ear. He talked to her, and she understood. She came to the edge of the bank, with soft little steps because she was afraid. But Gregorio Cortez kept talking to her and talking to her, and finally she jumped. She jumped far out and into the dark water below, she and Gregorio Cortez.

The other bank was not so high. Gregorio Cortez took out his *reata* and he lassoed a stump high on the bank. He climbed up the rope and got a stick, and with the stick he worked on

the bank as fast as he could, for he could hear the racket of
the dogs. The ground was soft, and he knocked off part of the
top and made something like a slope. Then he pulled and talked
until the mare came up the bank to where he was. After that
they rested up a bit and waited for the Rangers. Up they came
with their dogs to the spot where the mare had jumped. Then
Cortez fired a shot in the air and yelled, "I am Gregorio Cortez!"

And he rode away, leaving them standing there on the other
side, because none of them was brave enough to do what he
had done.

He rode on and on, and sometimes they chased him and
sometimes he stood and fought. And every time he fought he
would kill him a Ranger or two. They chased him across the
Arroyo del Cíbolo and into an oak grove, and there they made
him a corral. Then they sent the dogs away and sat down to
wait, for they wanted to catch him asleep. Gregorio Cortez
thought for a little while what he should do. Then he made his
mare lie down and he began talking to himself in different
voices, as if he were many men. This made the Rangers say
to one another, "There is a whole army of men with Gregorio
Cortez." So they broke up their corral and went away, because
they did not think there were enough of them to fight Gregorio
Cortez and all the men he had. And Gregorio Cortez rode away,
laughing to himself.

He kept riding on and on, by day and by night, and if he
slept the little mare stood guard and she would wake him up
when she heard a noise. He had no food or cigarettes, and his
ammunition was running low. He was going along a narrow
trail with a high barbed wire fence on one side and a nopal
thicket on the other, and right before he hit a turn he heard
horses ahead. The first man that came around the turn ran into
Gregorio Cortez with his pistol in his hand. There was a whole
line of others behind the first, all armed with rifles, but they
had to put those rifles away. Then Gregorio Cortez knocked
over a tall nopal plant with his stirrup and made just enough

room for his mare to back into while the Rangers filed by. He stopped the last one and took away his tobacco, matches, and ammunition. And then he rode away.

He rode on to La Grulla, and he was very thirsty because he had not had water in a long time, and the mare was thirsty too. Near La Grulla there was a dam where the vaqueros watered their stock. But when Gregorio Cortez got there, he saw twenty armed men resting under the trees that grew close to the water. Gregorio Cortez stopped and thought what he could do. Then he went back into the brush and began rounding up cattle, for this was cattle country and steers were everywhere. Pretty soon he had two hundred head and he drove them to water and while the cattle drank he and his mare drank too. After he finished, some of the Rangers resting under the trees came over and helped him get the herd together again, and Gregorio Cortez rode off with the herd, laughing to himself.

He rode on and on until he came to Cotulla, near the Rio Grande. But the little mare was tired now, and she began to limp. Gregorio Cortez rode into a thicket, and the Rangers made him a corral. But once in the brush Gregorio Cortez unsaddled the mare and tied her to a coma tree, and he patted her and talked to her for a long while. Then he slipped away, and the Rangers didn't see him because they were waiting for him to come riding out. They waited for three days and finally they crept in and found only the mare.

In the meantime Gregorio Cortez walked into town. He mixed with the Mexicans there, he sat on the station platform and listened to other men while they talked of all the things that Gregorio Cortez had done. Then he went to a store and bought himself some clothes and walked out of the town. That sort of man was Gregorio Cortez. They don't make them like him any more.

He had only three cartridges left, one for one pistol and two for the other. So he walked into El Sauz and tried to buy

some but they did not sell cartridges there. Then he thought of
trying some of the houses, and he chose one in which there was
a pretty girl at the door because he knew it would be easier if
he talked to a girl.

The girl was alone, and she invited him into the house.
When he asked for ammunition she said, "My father has taken
it all. He is out looking for a man named Gregorio Cortez."

Gregorio Cortez was embarrassed because he could see that
the girl knew who he was. But she did not let on and neither
did he. She gave him coffee and he stayed at the house for a
while, and when he left she told him how to get to the Rio
Grande by the quickest way.

Now all the people along the river knew that Gregorio
Cortez was on the Border and that he would soon cross, but
no one told the sheriffs what they knew. And Gregorio walked
on, in his new clothes, looking like an ordinary man, but the
people he met knew he was Gregorio Cortez. And he began
to talk to people along the way.

Soon he met a man who told him, "You'll be on the other
side of the river tonight, Gregorio Cortez. Things will be all
right with you then."

"I suppose they will," said Gregorio Cortez.

"But not for your brother," the man said. "He died in the
jail last night."

"He was badly wounded," said Gregorio Cortez. "It was his
lot to die."

"They beat him before he died," the man said.

This was the first news that Gregorio Cortez had heard, and
it made him thoughtful.

He walked on, and he met another man who said, "Your
mother is in the jail, Gregorio Cortez."

"Why?" said Gregorio Cortez.

"Because she is your mother," the man said. "Your wife is
there too, and so are your little sons."

Gregorio Cortez thought this over, and he walked on. Pretty

soon he met another man who said, "Gregorio Cortez, your own people are suffering, and all because of you."

"Why should my own people suffer?" said Gregorio Cortez. "And why because of me?"

"You have killed many Rangers," the man said. "They cannot catch you, so they take it out on people like you. Lots of men have been shot and beaten because they were your people. But you will be safe, Gregorio Cortez; you will cross the river tonight."

"I did not know these things," said Gregorio Cortez.

And he decided to turn back, and to give himself up to the Governor of the State so that his own people would not suffer because of him.

He turned and walked back until he came to a place called Goliad, where he met eleven Mexicans, and among them there was one who called himself his friend. This man was a vaquero named El Teco, but Judas should have been his name. Gregorio Cortez was thirsty, and he came up to the eleven Mexicans to ask for water, and when El Teco saw Gregorio Cortez he thought how good it would be if he could get the thousand dollar reward. So he walked up to Cortez and shook his hand and told the others, "Get some water for my friend Gregorio Cortez."

Then El Teco asked Gregorio Cortez to let him see the pistols he had, and said he would get him some ammunition. Gregorio Cortez smiled, because he knew. But he handed over the guns to El Teco, and El Teco looked at them and put them in his own *morral*. Then El Teco called the sheriffs to come and get Gregorio Cortez.

When Gregorio Cortez saw what El Teco had done, he said to him, "A man can only be what God made him. May you enjoy the reward."

But El Teco did not enjoy the reward, though the sheriffs gave him the money, one thousand dollars in silver, more than a *morral* could hold. He did not enjoy it because he could not spend it anywhere. If he went to buy a taco at the market place, the taco vendor would tell him that tacos were worth two thousand dollars gold that day. People cursed him in the streets and wished that he would be killed or die. So El Teco became very much afraid. He buried the money and never spent it, and he never knew peace until he died.

When the sheriffs came to arrest Gregorio Cortez, he spoke to them and said, "I am not your prisoner. I will be the prisoner only of the Governor of the State."

The sheriffs saw that he was in the right, so they went with him all the way to the Capital, and Cortez surrendered himself to the Governor of the State.

Then they put Cortez in jail, and all the Americans were glad because they no longer were afraid. They got together and they tried to lynch him. Three times they tried, but they could not lynch Gregorio Cortez.

And pretty soon all the people began to see that Gregorio Cortez was in the right, and they did not want to lynch him any more. They brought him gifts to the jail, and one day one of the judges came and shook the hand of Gregorio Cortez and said to him, "I would have done the same."

But Gregorio Cortez also had many enemies, for he had killed many men, and they wanted to see him hanged. So they brought him to trial for killing the Major Sheriff of the County of El Carmen. The lawyer that was against him got up and told the judges that Cortez should die because he had killed a man. Then Gregorio Cortez got up, and he spoke to them.

"Self-defense is allowed to any man," said Gregorio Cortez. "I killed the sheriff and I am not sorry, for he killed my brother. He spilled my brother's blood, which was also my blood. And he tried to kill me too. I killed the Major Sheriff defending my right."

And Gregorio Cortez talked for a long time to the judges, telling them about their own law. When he finished even the lawyer who was against him at the start was now for him. And all the judges came down from their benches and shook hands with Gregorio Cortez.

The judges said, "We cannot kill this man."

They took Gregorio Cortez all over the state, from town to town, and in each town he was tried before the court for the killing of a man. But in every court it was the same. Gregorio Cortez spoke to the judges and he told them about the law, and he proved that he had the right. And each time the judges said, "This man was defending his right. Tell the sheriffs to set him free."

And so it was that Gregorio Cortez was not found guilty of any wrong because of the sheriffs he had killed. And he killed many of them, there is no room for doubt. No man has killed more sheriffs than did Gregorio Cortez, and he always fought alone. For that is the way the real men fight, always on their own. There are young men around here today, who think that they are brave. Dangerous men they call themselves, and it takes five or six of them to jump a fellow and slash him in the arm. Or they hide in the brush and fill him full of buckshot as he goes by. They are not men. But that was not the way with Gregorio Cortez, for he was a real man.

The enemies of Gregorio Cortez got together and said to each other, "What are we going to do? This man is going free after killing so many of our friends. Shall we kill him ourselves? But we would have to catch him asleep, or shoot him in the back, because if we meet him face to face there will be few of us left."

Then one of them thought of the little sorrel mare, and there they had a plan to get Gregorio Cortez. They brought him back to court, and the lawyer who was against him asked, "Gregorio Cortez, do you recognize this mare?"

"I do," said Gregorio Cortez. "And a better little mare there never was."

Then the lawyer asked him, "Have you ridden this mare?"

And Gregorio Cortez answered, "She carried me all the way

from El Carmen to the Border, a distance of maybe 500 miles."

Then the lawyer asked him, "Is this mare yours?"

And Gregorio Cortez saw that they had him, but there was nothing he could do because he was an honest man and he felt that he must tell the truth. He said no, the mare did not belong to him.

Then the judges asked Gregorio Cortez, "Is this true, Gregorio Cortez? Did you take this mare that did not belong to you?"

And Gregorio Cortez had to say that the thing was true.

So they sentenced Gregorio Cortez, but not for killing the sheriffs, as some fools will tell you even now, when they ought to know better. No, not for killing the sheriffs but for stealing the little sorrel mare. The judge sentenced him to 99 years and a day. And the enemies of Gregorio Cortez were happy then, because they thought he would be in prison for the rest of his life.

But Gregorio Cortez did not stay in prison long. Inside of a year he was free, and this is the way it came about. Every year at Christmastime, a pretty girl can come to the Governor of the State and ask him to give her a prisoner as a Christmas present. And the Governor then has to set the prisoner free and give him to the girl. So it happened to Cortez. One day President Lincoln's daughter visited the prison, and she saw Gregorio Cortez. As soon as she saw him she went up and spoke to him.

"I am in love with you, Gregorio Cortez," President Lincoln's daughter said, "and if you promise to marry me I will go to the Governor next Christmas and tell him to give you to me."

Gregorio Cortez looked at President Lincoln's daughter, and he saw how beautiful she was. It made him thoughtful, and he did not know what to say.

"I have many rich farms," President Lincoln's daughter said. "They are all my own. Marry me and we will farm together."

Gregorio Cortez thought about that. He could see himself already like a German, sitting on the gallery full of ham and beer and belching and breaking wind while a half-dozen little blond cockroaches played in the yard. And he was tempted. But then he said to himself, "I can't marry a Gringo girl. We would not make a matching pair."

So he decided that President Lincoln's daughter was not the woman for him, and he told her, "I thank you very much; I cannot marry you at all."

But President Lincoln's daughter would not give up. She went to the Governor and said, "I would like to have a prisoner for Christmas."

And the Governor looked at her and saw she was a pretty girl, so he said, "Your wish is granted. What prisoner do you want?"

And President Lincoln's daughter said, "I want Gregorio Cortez."

The Governor thought for a little while and then he said, "That's a man you cannot have. He's the best prisoner I got."

But President Lincoln's daughter shook her head and told him, "Don't forget that you gave your word."

"So I did," the Governor said, "and I cannot go back on it."

And that was how Gregorio Cortez got out of prison, where he had been sentenced to 99 years and a day, not for killing the sheriffs, as some fools will tell you, but for stealing the little sorrel mare. Gregorio Cortez kept his word, and he did not marry President Lincoln's daughter, and when at last she lost her hopes she went away to the North.

Still the enemies of Gregorio Cortez did not give up. When they heard that he was getting out of prison they were scared and angry, and they started thinking of ways to get revenge. They got a lot of money together and gave it to a man who worked in the prison, and this man gave Gregorio Cortez a slow poison just before he got out of jail.

As soon as his friends saw him they said to each other, "This man is poisoned. He will not last the year."

And so it was. He did not last the year. He died of the slow poison they gave him, because his enemies did not want to see him free.

And that was how Gregorio Cortez came to die. He's buried in Laredo some place, or maybe it's Brownsville, or Matamoros, or somewhere up above. To tell the truth, I don't know. I don't know the place where he is buried any more than the place where he was born. But he was born and lived and died, that I do know. And a lot of Rangers could also tell you that.

So does the *corrido;* it tells about Gregorio Cortez and who he was. They started singing the *corrido* soon after he went to jail, and there was a time when it was forbidden in all the United States, by order of the President himself. Men sometimes got killed or lost their jobs because they sang "El Corrido de Gregorio Cortez." But everybody sang it just the same, because it spoke about things that were true.

Now it is all right to sing "El Corrido de Gregorio Cortez," but not everybody knows it any more. And they don't sing it as it used to be sung. These new singers change all the old songs a lot. But even so, people still remember Gregorio Cortez. And when a good singer sings his song—good and loud and clear—you can feel your neck-feathers rise, and you can see him standing there, with his pistol in his hand.

The Child Ballad in the Middle West and Lower Mississippi Valley

BROWNIE McNEIL

BEFORE THE YEAR 1882 there was no complete collection of traditional ballads in the English language. Francis James Child began the publication of his collected ballads in that year, and when completed in 1898 the collection consisted of five volumes containing 305 traditional ballads. By no means representing all the ballads in the English language, these are the "popular" (traditional or folk) ballads of England, the majority of which were known to have existed in oral tradition before they were written down. Occasionally Child included a version of a ballad that had been circulated in printed form when there was evidence it had been borrowed from a traditional version, but generally the work is a collection of the ballads which were sung for many centuries by the mass of unlettered folk in England and Scotland.

In tribute to the definitive nature of Child's work, the term *Child ballad* is often used in the present day when one speaks of the traditional ballad of England and Scotland. Its traditional background distinguishes it from the *broadside ballad*, a type written in a pseudocultivated poetic style. A great number of the latter were ground out in the sixteenth and seventeenth centuries by professional hack writers, many of whom borrowed their subject matter from traditional ballads.

Ballads of both types were brought to America by immigrants from England and Scotland during the eighteenth and early nineteenth centuries. Balladry in America during this period thus was essentially in the same state as it was in England. People retained in memory and passed on from one generation to the next by oral transmission a large number of the traditional ballads later collected by Child, and they also read broadside ballads printed on sheets of cheap paper and sold by every printshop in the country. Some of these were importations from England; others were of local creation. A notation in Cotton Mather's diary registers his complaint about the corrupting effect of "foolish" songs and ballads "which the hawkers and peddlers carry to all parts of the country," while Benjamin Franklin commented on the popularity of printed ballads: "I have known a very numerous impression of Robin Hood songs go off in this province at two shillings per book in less than a twelfth month; when a small quantity of David psalms have laid on my hands above twice that time." The great national spirit that arose during the American Revolutionary War furnished subject matter for many broadside ballads, created at first on a high level but eventually degenerating into mere sniping between political figures.

Both types of ballads exerted a lasting influence on balladry in America. Whereas the broadside ballads written on timely and localized subjects were soon forgotten, the stereotyped broadside style left its imprint on later traditional American ballads, particularly the work ballads that came from various occupational groups. A number of ballads of English broadside origin became traditional in America: "The Jealous Lover" and "Nancy of Yarmouth," for example. The former is widely known in America under a variety of titles, among them "The Oxford Girl," "The Wexford Girl," and "The Waco Girl."

The older traditional ballads of British origin, which for convenience we call Child ballads, survived in considerable number as a part of the traditional literature of the eastern portion of the United States. The greatest concentration of these ballads has been found in rural communities in the areas inhabited by people of predominantly British ancestry: New England and the Appalachian Mountains. West of these two areas the Child ballad is less popular, whereas a number of ballads of English broadside origin have perpetuated themselves with the substitution of local place names—"The Unfortunate Rake," for example, which appears in the Southwest as "The Streets of Laredo" and in the Rocky Mountains as "Only A Miner Killed in the Breast."

Our object here is to investigate the Child ballad in the region wherein the decline in its popularity becomes noticeable. This area west of the Appalachians and east of the Great Plains might be called *the midregion of the United States* for convenience, but a more exact description would be *the Middle West and lower Mississippi Valley*. After discovering the degree of survival of Child ballads in the region, we shall examine a representative number of these ballads to determine the principal changes that have developed in them—changes which should indicate a trend applicable to all Child ballads found west of the Appalachians.

Professor H. M. Belden, one of the most industrious collectors of ballads in Missouri and the surrounding area, inquired some years ago into the types of change that have occurred in Child ballads there. In 1912, when the *Journal of American Folk Lore* published his article on this topic, "Balladry in America," he had discovered eighteen Child ballads in Missouri. An examination of these revealed two types of change: elements in earlier texts which might be considered morally offensive to sensitive persons had been omitted, and ballads which in English versions deal with supernatural phenomena had tended in their American versions to lose their supernatural characteristics.

Another student of the ballad, MacEdward Leach, finds four types of change occurring in Child ballads in America. As he makes no distinction among regions, we must assume that these changes are applicable to ballads in the entire United

States. Repeating the two types of change defined by Belden, Leach suggests in addition the possibility that earlier manners and customs "are rationalized and made familiar" and that still other changes have resulted from "just plain forgetting."[1] Though they are burdened with nebulous terminology, there is some validity in these latter two points, the first supported by examples of changes in vocabulary, the second a statement in loose terms of a trend toward fragmentation.

There is, as we shall see, ample justification for setting forth a fifth type of change: the conversion of tragic elements into comic and ridiculous situations. Found in abundance among the Child ballads of the region, this change can be associated more clearly with the cultural characteristics of the Middle West and lower Mississippi Valley than any of the other four types of change.

The changes that have occurred in Child ballads in America appear more clearly delineated in those found west of the Appalachians than among those collected in the eastern states; the latter may reflect one or more of the five types of change mentioned above, but not in such fashion as to indicate a general trend. It is in the region west of the mountains that the changes have become well established; it is here we can approach the British ballad with the knowledge that it has passed a long enough period of residence in America and has migrated over an area of sufficient breadth to permit ample opportunity for change under the impact of American civilization.

It is one thing to discover changes which have occurred in ballads of a certain region; it is quite another to establish the causes of such changes. There are two general factors to consider: time and place. MacEdward Leach believes that change "is a consequence more of time than of place. English ballads today show the same types of change as do American ballads." But to say that British ballads both in England and America have developed the same types of change primarily because of the element of time ignores the way ballads adapt themselves to localities through which they pass. The ballad scholar William J. Entwistle more accurately observes that from the sixteenth century onward the English ballad gradually took on the broadside style: "... English balladry was not one whit less active in that century, but it had taken on a new direction. The invention and application of printing was causing balladmongers to print their wares on broadsides."[2] He is aware that ballads brought to America from England, where they had already come under the influence of the broadside, developed still other versions as a result of their residence in the new land: "... English settlers in America took with them the debris of the national ballads.... Such ballads served as the models for new creations on the American continent ..."

A general survey of Child ballads found in the American midregion reveals that of the more than one hundred discovered in this country, fewer than half have migrated west of the Appalachians. The fold-in chart shows how many examples of each Child ballad have been found in the Middle West and lower Mississippi Valley by collectors who have done work of significant proportion among the informants of the region. (Many of the prominent ballad collectors of the United States are not listed, since such workers as Cecil Sharp, Dorothy Scarborough, and John H. Cox confined their collecting almost exclusively to the Appalachian Mountains, while Phillips Barry, to name another, concentrated his attention on New England and adjacent areas of Canada.)

The majority of the collectors represented on the chart have consistently named both the town (or the county) and the state in which they discovered each ballad. Most of them also indicate in the titles of their articles or books the geographical area in which they did their work; Albert H. Tolman, for example, deals with ballads collected in both Indiana and Kansas. From Louise Pound's *American Ballads and Songs*, which covers ballads from all parts of the United States, only

those ballads have been selected which were collected in the
region under examination; also, duplication has been avoided
in Miss Pound's case by a check of her other work cited,
"Folk-Songs of Nebraska."

The chart indicates that, including those ballads of which
very few examples have been discovered, a total of forty-nine
Child ballads have migrated to the midregion of the United
States, only 40.8 per cent of the 120 Child ballads reported
for the entire United States by Reed Smith.[3] So as to set forth
more clearly the pattern of ballad survival, we will distinguish
between ballads of general survival (five examples or more)
and those of limited survival (fewer than five examples). Each
of the nineteen ballads of limited survival has been discovered
by no more than two collectors. The remaining thirty ballads
of general survival are listed in Table I below. Since Reed
Smith's checklist of 120 ballads makes no attempt to distinguish between those of general and those of limited survival,
we have no sound basis on which to compare the midregion
to the entire country in this aspect.

Table I gives a reasonably accurate view of the popularity
of certain Child ballads over others. "Barbara Allen" (84)
heads the list with 81 examples found. Four other ballads are
shown with thirty or more examples each: "James Harris (The
Daemon Lover)" (243), 51; "Lord Thomas and Fair Annet"
(73), 49; "Lady Isabel and the Elf-Knight" (4), 34; and "Lord
Lovel" (75), 30. Such figures do more, however, than indicate
popularity ratings. They convey an important fact regarding
the ballads' movement westward: all of those most popular
in the midregion deal with tragic love.

It would be speculative to credit cultural traits of the region
with the popularity of the tragic love theme—which could not,
for example, have been influenced by the midwestern tendency
to reject ideas bearing the mark of European culture, and to
promote that which is the creation of the region itself. Ballads
on specifically British subjects did not survive in the American

TABLE I

SURVIVAL OF CHILD BALLADS IN THE AMERICAN MIDREGION

Child No.	Child Title	Examples Found
84	Barbara Allen	81
243	James Harris (The Daemon Lover)	51
73	Lord Thomas and Fair Annet	49
4	Lady Isabel and the Elf-Knight	34
75	Lord Lovel	30
10	The Twa Sisters	26
76	The Lass of Roch Royal	21
12	Lord Randal	20
74	Fair Margaret and Sweet William	20
200	The Gypsy Laddie	20
95	The Maid Freed from the Gallows	18
2	The Elfin Knight	16
155	Sir Hugh, or, The Jew's Daughter	16
286	The Golden Vanity	14
49	The Two Brothers	13
26	The Three Ravens	12
295	The Brown Girl	12
79	The Wife of Usher's Well	11
289	The Mermaid	11
53	Young Beichan	10
278	The Farmer's Curst Wife	10
68	Young Hunting	9
277	The Wife Wrapt in Wether's Skin	9
13	Edward	8
209	Geordie	8
274	Our Goodman	8
85	Lady Alice	7
7	Earl Brand	6
250	Henry Martyn	6
18	Sir Lionel	5

midregion. While the checklist of Child ballads in America lists "The Hunting of the Cheviot" (162), "The Bonny Earl of Murray" (181), and "Rob Roy" (225), they are not reported by any midwestern collectors. Ballads dealing with border warfare between the English and the Scotch failed to live. The Robin Hood ballads, too, did not appeal to folk who had their own outlaw heroes in Jesse James and Cole Younger.

Tragic love, on the other hand, offers no national theme to invite rejection, and its personal and place names are not of basic importance. Unattached to individual nations or localities, it is a subject with universal human appeal.

One is always on dangerous ground in attempting to explain traditional literature in terms of movements in formal literature of conscious authorship; but within the fringe literature, that which was produced for the nineteenth century's new mass of readers, there might have existed influences to affect the traditional ballad. During the first half of the century Romanticism was the prevailing movement in American literature and thought; tragic love was a prominent theme in the cheap narratives turned out in quantity to satisfy the literary tastes of the masses. Could the popularity of this theme in written literature have been responsible for its similar popularity in ballads? "Lord Lovel," for example, deals with a lover who goes on some mysterious journey "far countries for to see"; he returns to find his sweetheart dead of an unknown cause, and he dies of grief himself. But the life of Romanticism as a literary movement was but a fraction of the span of traditional balladry; and while Romanticism borrowed much of its subject matter from traditional literature, there is no evidence that it, in return, brought about any changes in traditional literature. There is the additional fact that Romanticism as a movement in formal literature came to an end during the 1860's, whereas the ballads with which we are dealing were not collected until fifty years or more later. If they had been influenced by movements in literature of formal authorship, these influences would be reflections not of Romanticism but of Realism and Naturalism, which held sway after Romanticism had ceased to exist.

A more logical explanation of the popularity of the tragic love theme in Child ballads of the midregion lies in facts more closely associated with traditional balladry. By 1800 the printed broadside of conscious authorship had had considerable effect on the ballad in England and particularly in America, where ballads even many centuries old were heavily influenced. Child emphasizes how frequently hack writers of broadsides in England borrowed their stories from traditional ballads, especially ballads of tragic love. Reed Smith cites broadside versions of each of the five most popular Child ballads listed in Table I. "Lord Thomas and Fair Annet" (73), for example, is shown to have been licensed as a broadside by one L'Estrange between the years 1663 and 1685. Entwistle speaks of the exceptional influence of the broadside on the traditional ballad in America, mentioning the sentimental "Barbara Allen" as one of the most popular in this respect. MacEdward Leach points out that this ballad was frequently used as broadside material and remarks that such broadsides have often been reintroduced into oral tradition. We might conclude that the frequent appearance in broadside form of Child ballads dealing with tragic love brought about also a great diffusion of the traditional forms of those same ballads.

By far the most successful collector shown on the fold-in chart, with forty separate Child ballads discovered, is Vance Randolph, who collected ballads and folksongs exclusively in the Ozarks. Of four large volumes resulting from his efforts, Volume I is devoted entirely to British ballads and songs from this locality. Randolph's nearest rival in total number of Child survivals discovered, H. M. Belden (with twenty-nine), likewise conducted much of his field collecting among Ozark people, although he did not devote his efforts to that locality exclusively. Six of the forty Child ballads discovered in the region by Randolph were not reported by any other collector, while three others in his group were listed by only one other collector. Such figures indicate that the Ozarks contain a greater concentration of Child ballad survivals than any other locality west of the Appalachians. The Ozarks were settled principally by immigrants from the Appalachians, who would undoubtedly have transported a relatively large number of Child ballads to their new locality.

The map below shows the distribution of Child ballads in
the Middle West and lower Mississippi Valley as reported by
collectors of the region. It does not purport to be a complete

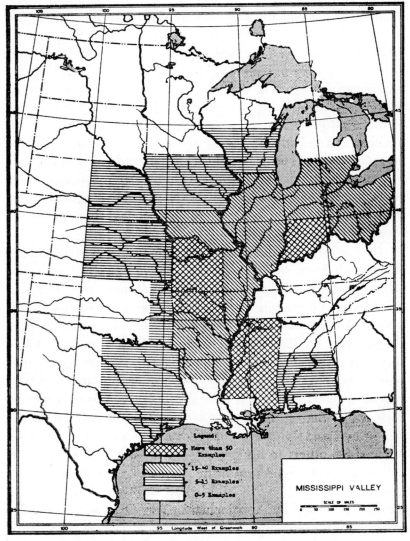

Distribution of Child Ballads in the Middle West
and Lower Mississippi Valley

representation of all Child ballads in the entire region, but only in those areas where collectors have been active. We must also take certain liberties with the actual geographical areas covered by the collectors. We know, for example, that Emelyn E. Gardner and Geraldine J. Chickering collected ballads only in southern Michigan, and that Earl C. Beck worked in the northern part of that state. Therefore on the map Michigan has been divided into two parts, each shaded according to the findings of the collectors. Even though a collector may have confined his activities to no more than a dozen communities, it would be reasonably accurate to shade the area in which he worked for an arbitrary distance of about one hundred and fifty miles around the actual focal point of his collecting. Thus, the southern half of Wisconsin has been shaded to represent the findings of Asher E. Treat. Mabel Major and William A. Owens collected Child ballads mainly northeast of the Colorado River in Texas and east of the ninety-eighth meridian; therefore that area has been shaded to correspond with the number of ballads they report.

Collectors of course work with varying effectiveness. For example, A. P. Hudson turned up a concentration of Child ballads in the midsection of Mississippi, while Byron Arnold located only seven in mid-Alabama, an area of similar social and economic conditions where we would expect to find as many ballads. The fact that neither Kentucky nor Tennessee is shaded on the map does not mean that these states are entirely devoid of Child ballads, but rather that collectors there have done the majority of their work in the mountains, an area outside the map's scope. No collector appears to have worked west of the mountains exclusively in Kentucky and Tennessee. Minnesota, North Dakota, and South Dakota, with populations largely drawn from northern Europe, would be expected to yield but few Child ballads. Collectors apparently have not investigated these states; they have also ignored Oklahoma.

As the map reveals, west of the Mississippi Child ballads
have declined rapidly in popularity, with the larger part of this
area showing fewer than fifteen examples and much of it
falling below five examples. An exception is the Ozark Mountains, a major depository of ballads which is surrounded, however, by areas of declining interest.

Child ballads are also seen to have remained most abundant
in the areas where the principal economic unit has been the
small, self-sufficient farm tilled by people firmly rooted in the
soil. Farm families in such areas (generally east of the ninety-
eighth meridian) could spend their lives on one piece of land,
blessed with secure agricultural conditions. When they moved
westward out on the plains, however, they encountered for the
first time in their experience a land that was treeless and water-
less, a life that was unstable and insecure. In this new environment the Child ballad all but disappeared. Albert H. Tolman,
for example, has reported very few ballads from Kansas. John
A. Lomax, who collected ballads among the cow camps of
West Texas and in the open range country of New Mexico,
found there fewer than five Child ballads. Louise Pound
reports the greatest number of Child ballads (approximately
twenty) from any plains area. In general, however, relatively
few Child ballads are known to have survived west of the
ninety-eighth meridian.

Another area in which they failed to live is northern Michigan. When Earl C. Beck collected the songs of the Michigan
lumberjacks, he found but one example of a Child ballad,
"The Farmer's Curst Wife" (278).

1. Rejection of Morally Offensive Elements

We have observed that Child ballads in the midregion of
the United States developed a variety of changes—one such
being their loss, or glossing over, of elements which might be
morally offensive. While the tendency to eliminate such elements is present in mountain ballads also, it becomes an innate

property of those of the midregion, where one finds a number
of ballads which formerly developed a narrative around such
themes as adultery, incest, and murder provoked by sexual
promiscuity, but which in their present form have excluded
those themes or have hidden them in vague language. The
subordination of immoral elements has often been accompanied
by emphasis on other elements which in the earlier versions
were insignificant. This sort of modification might be explained
in terms of the nineteenth-century change both in England and
America in social attitudes toward women, especially as
reflected in the speech of gentlemen in the company of their
ladies. Much of what later came to be called *Victorian manners*
sprang from social taboos against the discussion in mixed company of any matter related to sex, with consequent substitution
of "polite" terms for others considered too crude for feminine
ears—*limbs* for *legs; in a family way* for *pregnant.* In such an
age the "purity" of women exerted a far greater influence on
the daily lives of people than in the preceding century; and
this influence was especially strong on the settlers of the American midregion, where men were expected to conduct themselves in the presence of women with the utmost propriety.
This restraint was encouraged by the work of revivalist
preachers like Peter Cartwright who roamed the Mississippi
and Ohio Valley states and railed at every camp meeting
against sinful ways.

Ballads migrating to the Midwest and lower Mississippi
Valley came under the influence of the region's pervasive spirit
of propriety and were made to conform to the sensibilities of
the people. Those which appear most extensively altered in
this respect are the ballads which formerly dealt with incest:
"The Two Brothers" (49), for example, which in Child versions
is closely associated with "Lizzie Wan" (51) and "The Sheath
Knife" (16), the former describing brother-sister incest on the
ordinary folk level, the latter that between a prince and a
princess. Child's version *A* of "Edward" (13) might also be

associated with this motif. The only explanation given for the
murder in this ballad is the cutting of a willow wand "that
would never been a tree," a phrase continued in the nine
examples of "The Two Brothers" found in the American midregion, although there is not the slightest suggestion of incest
in the latter, as there is in Child's version *A* of "The Two
Brothers":

> "And what will I say to my sister dear,
> Should she chance to say, 'Willie, whar's John?' "
> "Oh, say that he's to England gone,
> To buy her a wedding ring."[4]

Mrs. Nancy Brewster of Oakland City, Indiana, contributed a
version in which the murderer, as in "Lizzie Wan," vows to
escape the father's vengeance by taking a ship:

> "What will you tell your dear papa
> When he comes home in the evening?"
> "I'll set my foot on yonder ship
> And sail away to sea."[5]

The question-and-answer exchange between the dying brother
and his murderer ends with the matter of what to tell their
father and mother, no mention whatsoever being made of the
sister, as in the Child ballad. This same pattern is used in
another example obtained by Paul G. Brewster in Indiana.
The story is ended rather abruptly in both ballads with the
plan to elude the father, and with no motive for the murder
given. An example collected by H. M. Belden in Columbia,
Missouri, introduces the sister in the question-and-answer
sequence, but the reply contains no reference to incest:

> "Oh brother, oh brother, when you go home
> My sister will ask for me;
> Tell her I'm down in Dublin town
> Sleeping beneath the churchyard tree."[6]

Louise Pound gives an example of this ballad entitled "Two
Little Boys." In spite of the title, one of the principals is old

enough to have a sweetheart, who is substituted for the sister. Thus the incestuous element is converted entirely to a normal relationship between a boy and his sweetheart; there is not even rivalry between the boys for her hand. The ballad has also changed the cause of death from murder to an accident occurring while the two boys are enjoying a playful wrestling match:

> They wrestled up, they wrestled down,
> They wrestled around and around,
> And a little penknife run through John's pocket,
> And he received a deadly wound.
>
> "Oh, what shall I tell your true love, John,
> If she inquires about you?"
> "O, tell her I'm dead and lying in my grave,
> Way out in Idaho."[7]

The reference to Idaho is given apparently for no purpose other than rhyme, but it serves to place the ballad as to region and approximate date. An example discovered by A. P. Hudson in Pine Valley, Mississippi, entitled "The Cruel Brother," is a much briefer narrative and mentions neither sister, wife, nor sweetheart.

Through the long history of "The Two Brothers" and "Edward," the two ballads have exchanged many narrative elements. Some English versions of "Edward" introduce the incest theme, making the sister the victim of the murder; but this element does not appear in any of the eight examples of the ballad found in the American midregion. An example of "Edward" recorded by Hudson (also entitled "The Cruel Brother," although the informant was not the one supplying the example of Child 49 above) adheres to the more common pattern found in Child A, picturing the murderer, Son Davie, with a wife and children. The latter appear also in the example published in William A. Owens' collection. In these two examples of the ballad, as well as in most versions found in the southern Appalachians, the murderer proposes to take his

wife and children aboard ship and escape with them across
the sea, contrary to the Child version A, which makes the wife
a party to the murder and strongly suggests adultery.

The ballad "Sir Hugh, or, The Jew's Daughter" (155) in
certain English versions implies that the Jew's daughter entices
the boy into her house to introduce him to sexual pleasures,
the enticement being symbolized by the apple and the cherry
—figures found in many versions of the ballad both in England
and in America. Four examples encountered in the American
midregion make use of the blood-red cherry image, but its
connotation of sexual invitation is only implied, as in the
English versions. Sexual immorality in this ballad would appear
to be only one among a variety of motives inspiring the Jewess
to her crime. In some versions she is an agent acting for the
entire family; these embody a religious motive, the reprisal
of the Jews for torments suffered at the hands of the Christians.
An example collected by Albert H. Tolman in Warren, Indiana,
heightens the mystery of the forbidden territory of the Jew's
garden with the phrase, "Where no one was darst to go." The
action is brought back to reality, however, when the Jew's
daughter shows the young boy a thing so worldly as a "yellow
dish apple" before revealing the red cherry:

> At first they tossed their ball too high,
> And then again too low,
> Till over in the Jewish garden it fell,
> Where no one was darst to go, go, go,
> Where no one was darst to go.
>
> At first she showed him a yellow dish apple,
> And a gay gold ring,
> And then a cherry as red as blood,
> To entice this little boy in, in, in,
> To entice this little boy in.[8]

The cherry-and-apple symbolism does not appear in all English versions, so it cannot be claimed on this basis alone that
the immoral element was rejected only when the ballad ar-

rived in the midregion. The English versions which do mention
the fruit emphasize the act of showing, whereas the American
examples do not. An example collected by Paul G. Brewster in
Indiana has changed the imagery from the act of display to a
literal pulling of the fruit off trees:

> She pulled him off a green apple,
> She offered it to him;
> She pulled him off a blood-red cherry,
> And that enticed him in.

Several English versions of "Young Hunting" (68) begin
with a direct invitation issued to Young Hunting by his mistress
to spend the night, followed by his refusal and murder. The
example collected by A. P. Hudson in Mississippi has rejected
the theme of sexual immorality by shifting the opening to a
point after the murder has been committed—and then indicating that Young Hunting's murderer is his wife. Thus the ballad
has become another story of a wife who lays her unfaithful
husband low, murder being a much less heinous crime in
Mississippi, evidently, than cohabiting without benefit of marriage. This ballad is interesting too for its complete invention
of a question-and-answer sequence, this time between father-
in-law and daughter-in-law:

> She was walking in the garden one day,
> . . . .
> And whom should she see but her own father-in-law,
> Saying, "Daughter, where's my son?"
>
> "He's been a-hunting these three long days,
> I expect him home tomorrow;
> But if he does not return home again
> My heart will break with sorrow."[9]

The action continues with the traditional stanzas between the
lady and her talkative parrot borrowed from "Lady Isabel and
the Elf-Knight" (4). In the final lines the lady is punished:

This lady and her merry maidens all
Were hung next market day.

The ballad of "Little Musgrave and Lady Barnard" (81) is
a narrative involving adultery. Why is it, then, that we find it
at all among the Child ballads of the American midregion,
where direct references to adultery were not considered fit
subject matter for mixed company? The ballad was not popular
in the region, as a matter of fact: only six examples have been
reported, and three of these are from a single area, the Ozarks.
Also, there is in some examples an attempt to gloss over the
bedroom scene, with rather self-conscious results. The handling
of this scene in H. M. Belden's example from Missouri is
particularly awkward:

From that they fell to hugging and kissing,
And from that they fell to sleep;
And next morning when they woke at the break of day
Lord Arnold stood at their feet.

In emphasizing so pointedly that the couple passed directly
from kissing to sleep the singer of this ballad probably was
making an attempt to avoid direct mention of the adulterous
situation. The result of the ruse, however, is to call greater
attention to the matter than ever was done in the English versions, wherein adultery is subordinate to the main point: Lord
Barnard's hasty action and subsequent remorse over killing the
unlucky pair. In the example collected by Gardner and Chickering in Michigan, the attempt to gloss over the immorality is
less comic but no more convincing:

Long and sweet they conversed that night,
And at last they both fell asleep;
And when they awoke it was broad daylight,
Lord Valley he stood at their feet.[10]

The English versions of "The Gypsy Laddie" (200) present
an adulterous situation in which the gypsy charms the wife of

a nobleman with his sweet singing and persuades her to run away with him, forsaking husband, baby, and home. Some mid-region examples of this ballad reduce the magnitude of the sin by making the lady an unmarried young girl. For this purpose, as in an example collected by A. P. Hudson in Mississippi, a stanza is invented to convey an idea of her youth and giddiness:

> "How old are you, my pretty little miss,
> How old are you, my honey?"
> She answered him with a "He, ho, ha,
> I'll be sixteen next Sunday."

Another stanza from the same example all but eliminates any suggestion of immoral behavior, showing the gypsy as a man of honorable intentions who asks the young lady to be his wife:

> "If you will come and go with me
> And be my wife forever,
> I'll swear by the sword that hangs by my side
> You'll never want for money."

Of the nine examples of "The Gypsy Laddie" found in the region, six contain some reference to the extreme youth of the lady. Most of them, however, place her in some sort of married status prior to the gypsy's courtship. An example collected by Charles Neely in southern Illinois, like that described above from Hudson's collection, presents the girl in a youthful role, apparently in a subtle attempt to lighten the seriousness of her behavior. The courtship scene is described in a pair of stanzas which picture her as the essence of silliness:

> "How old are you, my pretty little miss?
> How old are you, my honey?"
> She answered me with a smile and a kiss,
> "I'll be seventeen next Sunday."

> "Will you go with me, my pretty little miss?
> Will you go with me, my honey?"
> She answered me with a smile and a kiss,
> "I'll go with you next Sunday."[11]

The American ballads which tell the story of Child's "The Elfin Knight" (2) have descended from older versions narrating the successful efforts of a maiden to ward off the charms of an evil elf-knight or an equally malicious knight in human form. Whether elf or human being, the knight in some Child versions attempts to seduce the maiden by casting a spell over her. American versions have mostly done away with elf and knight alike and have developed two separate narrative motifs, neither of which continues the element of seduction. One deals with a comic situation in which the girl avoids the attentions of an old man by assigning him impossible tasks to perform, as in the example from Missouri included in Belden's collection:

> Tell him to deed me an acre of land
> Between salt water and sea land.
>
> Tell him to plow it with a sheep's horn
> And seed it down with three grains of corn.
>
> Tell him to reap it with a pen knife
> And haul it in with a single span of mice.
>
> Tell him to put it in yonder barn,
> That never was built since Adam was born.
>
> Tell him to build me a ship of brick
> And come sailing over the deep.
>
> Tell the old fool when he's done this work,
> To bring me the land and I'll give him the shirt.

The other motif found in American examples of "The Elfin Knight" is that of courtship between a young man and a maiden, with the customary happy ending. This type has retained the feature of the impossible tasks, in this case imposed by each party upon the other so that each can test the degree of the other's love. Thus, what formerly was a tale of evil seduction has become a story of innocent courtship. Of the sixteen examples of this ballad found in America, the majority develop this style of narrative. The typical ending is shown in the example discovered by Paul G. Brewster in Indiana:

> Just tell that gent if he's done his work,
> Ly flum a lum a licker aloma,
> He can call tonight and get his shirt,
> Tum a tiest tum a tiste tuma tinest
> Ly flum a lum a licker aloma.

An important fact is that none of the examples discovered in the Middle West and lower Mississippi Valley develops the narrative according to the earlier motif, in which a maiden protects herself against the conjurings of an evil seducer.

2. *Rationalization of the Supernatural*

A second characteristic of Child ballads west of the Appalachians is their exclusion of any serious treatment of supernatural elements. Ballads which in their earlier English versions dealt with such beings out of medieval lore as elves, devils, and ghosts now limit themselves to characters cast in human form. The elfin knight is no longer either an elf or a knight; ghosts no longer appear, and violins which formerly talked and accused the perpetrators of a crime have been dropped. As a matter of fact, the tendency to eliminate the supernatural altogether or to rationalize supernatural elements into realistic elements is characteristic of British ballads generally in the whole of America; but it is in the region west of the Appalachians that we find this characteristic most clearly established.

In the eastern portion of the country one does find in Child ballads a residue of the supernatural which is absent, except in isolated instances, among ballads found west of the mountains. For example, "The Suffolk Miracle" (272), which deals with an adventure between a living person and a ghost, appears in two major collections of mountain ballads, Sharp's *English Folk Songs from the Southern Appalachians* and Cox's *Folk-Songs of the South*. It has been found in only one instance west of the Appalachians. Vance Randolph records an incomplete example in the Ozarks.

One of the best-known ghosts in British balladry is that of

Lady Margaret, which appears at the foot of Sweet William's bed on the night of his wedding to another. The ghost is a vital element in most English versions of "Fair Margaret and Sweet William" (74), and it appears in numerous examples of the same ballad in the eastern portion of the United States. Sharp gives five full texts, three of which have retained the supernatural element; Cox presents seven examples, of which no fewer than five make direct mention of Margaret's ghost. By contrast, out of a total of twenty examples of the ballad listed by collectors in the American midregion, eighteen either bring Margaret to the foot of Sweet William's bed as a live person, or eliminate the scene altogether.

It is interesting to note how few Child ballads embodying supernatural elements have survived in the Middle West and

TABLE II

Survival of Supernatural Ballads in the American Midregion

Child No.	Title	Smith	Midregion
2	The Elfin Knight	*	
4	Lady Isabel and the Elf-Knight	*	*
10	The Twa Sisters	*	*
29	The Boy and the Mantle		
34	Kemp Owyne		
35	Allison Gross		
39	Tam Lin	*	
40	The Queen of Elfan's Nourice	*	
42	Clerk Colvill		
43	Broomfield Hill	*	
44	The Twa Magicians		
59	Sir Aldingar		
74	Fair Margaret and Sweet William	*	*
77	Sweet William's Ghost	*	
78	The Unquiet Grave	*	
79	The Wife of Usher's Well	*	*
214	The Braes of Yarrow	*	
255	Willie's Fatal Visit		
265	The Knight's Ghost		
272	The Suffolk Miracle	*	*
278	The Farmer's Curst Wife	*	*

lower Mississippi Valley. Table II above, while indicating that supernatural themes were not popular with ballad singers of the region, cannot be interpreted as explanation of why certain ballads survived in the region while others failed to do so; the presence or absence of supernatural elements is not in itself any answer. Of twenty-one Child ballads in which supernatural elements figure prominently, thirteen (asterisked under "Smith") appear on Reed Smith's checklist of Child ballads in America, while only seven (asterisked under "Midregion") have been collected in the Middle West and lower Mississippi Valley.

To what degree have the seven ballads surviving in the midregion preserved supernatural elements in their narratives? We may find the answer to this question by examining several of these ballads to see what remains of their ghosts and elves.

"The Elfin Knight" (2) is a popular ballad in the American midregion, some fourteen examples having been reported under such titles as "The Cambric Shirt," "A True Lover of Mine," "The Two Lovers," "Rosemary and Thyme." Child's version A of this ballad describes a contest of wits between a maiden and an elf-knight who intends to seduce her, first attracting her interest by blowing on his horn:

> He blowes it east, he blowes it west,
> He blowes it where he lyketh best.

The notes from the horn make her desire him, and he appears at her bedside. Then begins the assignment of impossible tasks by both parties, at the end of which she has outwitted him by making him admit to having a wife and children. She then realizes his evil intentions and says:

> "My maidenhead I'll then keep still,
> Let the elphin knight do what he will."

In none of the versions of "The Elfin Knight" found west of the

Appalachians does the male character appear in his supernatural form; the story has become one of courtship either
between two lovers who test each other's love, or between a
maiden and an old man who is assigned impossible tasks to
discourage him. In a version from Princeton, Indiana, collected
by Paul G. Brewster, the lovers address an unnamed third
party:

> I want her to make me a cambric shirt,
> Rivers and seas are merry in time,
> With very fine needle and very coarse work,
> Then she shall be a true lover of mine.
>
> Go tell him to plant an acre of land,
> Rivers and seas are merry in time,
> Between the salt sea and the dry sand,
> Then he shall be a true lover of mine.

Another version found by Brewster in Aurora, Indiana, has
omitted the courtship theme altogether. The young man
addresses his mother, assigns the usual impossible tasks, and
then bows out:

> Mother, make me a cambric shirt
> Fom a nomanee, cast nomanee,
> Without a stitch of needlework
> Keely ope, keely ope, patalai, patempali,
> Fom a nomanee, cast nomanee.
>
> Wash it out in an old dry well,
> *etc., etc.,*
> Where a drop of water never fell,
> *etc.*
>
> Hang it out on an old bush thorn,
> Where the sun never shone since Adam was born,
> *etc.*
> Mother, plant me an acre of corn,
> And plow it up with an old ram's horn,
> *etc.*
>
> Now, kind friends, my song is done,
> I hope I've not offended one,
> *etc.*

H. M. Belden presents a version from Missouri that invents a
messenger to carry the assignments back and forth:

> Are you a-going to London, sir?
> Fum a lum a castly ony,
> Just give my love to a little girl there,
> Tum a keetle, o keetle, o taly, *etc.*
>
> Tell her to make me a cambric shirt
> Without a needle or needler's work,
> *etc.*

The motif of the elf who charms a girl by blowing on his
horn appears also in early versions of "Lady Isabel and the Elf-
Knight" (4). In American versions both east and west of the
Appalachians the supernatural being has been replaced by a
realistic character in human form, usually unidentified until
the middle of the story when he makes his intentions known to
the maiden. The nearest American examples of this ballad
come to giving supernatural status to this seducer and murderer
is a suggestion of mysterious origin, as in a Georgia version
from Cecil Sharp's collection:

> There was a proper tall young man,
> And William was his name;
> He came away over the ragin' sea,
> He came a-courting me, O me,
> He came a-courting me.[12]

Another version found by Sharp in Virginia opens with strong
suggestion of enchantment, but there is no direct reference to
supernaturalism:

> He followed her up and he followed her down,
> He followed her to the room where she lay,
> And she had not the power to flee from his arms,
> Nor the tongue to answer Nay, Nay, Nay,
> Nor the tongue to answer Nay.

The murderer is identified as a knight in several eastern ver-

sions—a knight, however, with human characteristics, as in this
stanza from Mattawamkeag, Maine:

> I'll tell you of a false hearted knight
> Who courted a lady gay,
> And all that he wanted of this pretty fair maid
> Was to take her sweet life away.[13]

While the suggestion of mysterious origin and powers has continued among certain examples of this ballad, the majority of
the twenty-nine versions discovered in the midregion have lost
all references to supernatural origin. Most of them begin with
a direct order to the maiden to bring her parents' money, as in
the example collected by William A. Owens in a Texas community close to Louisiana:

> "Go bring me some of your father's gold
> And bring me your mother's fee.
> Oh, come, oh, come my Pretty Polly
> And go along with me."[14]

Child's versions *A* and *B* of "The Twa Sisters" (10) both
develop the motif of a violin which is made of the parts of a
drowned girl's body and is thus given magical properties
enabling it to accuse the girl's sister of the crime. Of the
eighteen versions of this ballad reported in the American midregion none has preserved this motif, the majority of them
developing instead a narrative in which a villainous miller
(or his son) fishes the drowning sister out of the millpond, robs
her of her rings, and pushes her in again. An example is Belden's
version from Tuscumbia, Missouri:

> "O miller, O miller, yonder comes a swan
> A-swimming down the old mill pond."
>
> The miller threw out his old grab hook
> And brought her safely from the brook.
>
> He robbed her of her golden ring
> And plunged her in the brook again.

They hung him on his own mill gate
For drownding of poor sister Kate.

The narrative of "The Wife of Usher's Well" (79) is so entirely dependent on a supernatural event that the ballad could hardly survive without it. The nine versions found in the American midregion (most of them entitled "The Three Little Babes") retain the theme of three dead children returning to visit their mother, but variations have developed to limit the supernatural element. The great air of mystery pervading the earlier Scottish version (Child A) has been dissipated into sentimentality, and a religious theme has replaced the supernatural motif, as in this version collected by Belden in Ballinger County, Missouri:

She prayed to God, if there be any God,
If there be any God on high,
To send her three little babes back home
That night or soon next day.

It being close to Christmas times,
When the nights was long and cool,
"Come home, come home, my three little babes,
Come running home again.

"Spread o'er the table bread and wine,
That my three little babes may dine."
"I cannot eat none of your bread,
Neither can I drink your wine.

"Tomorrow morn at eight o'clock
With my Savior I will dine."
"Spread o'er the bed the golden sheet,
That my three little babes may sleep."

"Cold clods, cold clods at my head and feet,
Cold clods at my head and feet;
The tears that flow from a mother's eyes
Will wet a winding sheet."

As pointed out above, most versions of "Fair Margaret and Sweet William" (74) found in the Appalachians retain the ghost feature of the Child originals, while only two collected west of the mountains make direct mention of a ghost. One of these is in the collection of Vance Randolph (who also, however, presents three additional examples of the ballad which omit the ghost); the other, discovered by Charles Neely in southern Illinois, describes the bedroom scene as follows:

> 'Twas at the silent midnight hour
> When all were fast asleep;
> In glided Margaret's grimly ghost,
> And stood at William's feet.

The version given by Randolph is similar:

> The day bein' gone an' the night comin' on
> When all men were asleep,
> Sweet William spied Lydia Margaret's ghost
> A-standin' at his bed's feet.[15]

This same scene is presented in two versions of the ballad recorded by Belden in Missouri, one collected by Paul G. Brewster in Indiana, and one found by A. P. Hudson in Mississippi. Lady Margaret wreaks a rather anticlimactic vengeance on Sweet William, in one of the Belden examples, by making him bow:

> She threw down her ivory comb,
> She just brushed back her hair;
> She went and she made Sweet William bow
> And no more did she go back there.

Brewster's example describes the bedroom scene in a stanza almost identical with those of Neely and Randolph, except that the live Lady Margaret comes "walking softly downstairs." In the Hudson version Sweet William dreams he sees Lady Margaret at his feet and is undone when he kisses her:

> The day being o'er and the time drawing near
> When all of the men were asleep,
> Sweet William dreamed Lady Maggie was there
> A-standing at his bed feet.

> The first he kissed was her pale cold cheek,
> The next was her dimpled chin;
> And last of all was her cold blue lips,
> That pierced his heart within.

This scene is undoubtedly a transfer of the dream episode which appears later in the narrative in Child versions.

The remaining examples of "Fair Margaret and Sweet William" omit the bedroom scene, most of them making use of some sort of substitute situation or reference, such as the disturbing dream in the Ohio example presented by Mary O. Eddy:

> The day was far spent and the night was coming on,
> When most of the men was at work;
> Sweet William he said he was troubled in his head
> By a dream that he dreampt that night.[16]

A number of examples that have omitted the ghost and bedroom scene altogether have substituted narrative elements from other ballads. One collected by Brewster introduces the scene from "Lord Thomas and Fair Annet" wherein Lady Margaret, having been counseled by her mother to stay at home, instead dresses herself in costly robes and rides through the town, where everyone takes her to be a queen.

Another ballad containing a supernatural element, "The Farmer's Curst Wife" (278), presents a comic situation, and in Child's versions the listener is not required to believe literally in the picture of the devil presented. Midregion examples make no substitute for the devil; it would be impossible to do without him, since the entire situation centers about his carting the old wife off to hell and the trouble he has with her there until he brings her back.

3. Changes in Poetic Imagery, Vocabulary, Verse Pattern

The Child ballads discovered in the Middle West and lower Mississippi Valley have undergone noticeable changes in

characteristics of poetic imagery, vocabulary, and verse pattern. The imagery which enriches British versions has been
modified to a style less stimulating to the imagination. The air
of great mystery typical of some Child originals has changed
into a more worldly, unexcited, matter-of-fact tone. The tense
drama of original scenes has been dissipated; there is frequent
indiscriminate transfer of dramatic situations between ballads
in America, and in their new settings they lose their former
forcefulness.

Vocabulary in numerous instances has undergone regional
adaptation. Place names or references have often been localized: in an example of "Barbara Allen" (84) from Illinois
Sweet William appears "from the western states," while in one
version of "The Two Brothers" (49) the murdered brother is
buried "way out in Idaho." Or an English name is generalized
—"London Town" becomes "Lasso Town" or "Scarlet Town,"
the latter appearing in numerous examples of "Barbara Allen."
Archaic terms are sometimes retained, but in pronunciations
indicating their meaning is lost on singers of the midregion.
In a version of "The Wife of Usher's Well" (79) from Missouri
the three babes are sent away "to learn the *garmuree*," the informant having missed entirely the import of the original word
grammaree. (An example of "The Two Brothers" (49), borrow-
ing this situation from "The Wife of Usher's Well," has the
boys sent to learn their *A, B, C.*) Then there are the frequent
substitutions of local colloquialisms for the more formal original
language, as in the case of the murderer in "Lady Isabel and
the Elf-Knight" (4) who tells Pretty Polly to "light off" her
horse (to dismount) in a version collected by H. M. Belden
in Missouri.

The verse pattern of Child ballads in the midregion has
generally become more flexible. Informants show little concern
for regularity of rhythm, and frequently depart radically from
the basic four-line ballad stanza alternating lines of iambic
tetrameter and iambic trimeter. The English versions are rela-

tively rigid in their stanzaic pattern, except for the occasional
introduction of an anapestic foot at the beginning of some line
other than the first; they are more consistent in maintaining the
alternating tetrameter and trimeter. Ballads of the midregion
often, for no apparent reason, annex a fifth line to a stanza
when all other stanzas in the ballad follow the regular four-line
pattern.

American ballads have a great affinity for nonsense refrains,
preserving and varying those of English versions of "The Elfin
Knight" (2), "The Twa Sisters" (10), and "The Three Ravens"
(26), while adding such a refrain to one ballad, "The Gypsy
Laddie" (200), whose British prototype possesses none. An
example of this last ballad found in Texas interrupts the narrative frequently for a refrain with separate stanzaic arrangement, beginning with "Rigga, digga, dingo, dingo, da."

Imagery in Child ballads of the region tends to be less suggestive than in the originals, with addition of explicit details
which British versions had left to the listener's imagination, as
in an example of "Lady Isabel and the Elf-Knight" (4) collected by Belden in Missouri:

> She handed him down her father's gold,
> Likewise her mother's too;
> Away they went to the stable door,
> Took choice of twenty and two.

The handling of gold and selection of horses were only implied,
not stated, in Child's versions. The seaside disrobing scene in
the same ballad evidences more fascination with detail:

> She pulled off the lily-white robe
> And delivered it up to him,
> For it was too fine and cost too much
> To rot in the bottom of the sea.

In a version of the same ballad found by Brewster in Evans-
ville, Indiana, we hear in the opening stanza the irritated voice

of the young lady complaining in very worldly tones of being
followed by a pest:

> He followed me up and he followed me around,
> And he followed me around all day;
> I had not the power to speak a word
> Or a tongue to answer, "Nay, O Nay,"
> Or a tongue to answer "Nay."

At one point the murderer is quite specific about the manner in
which his victim is to disrobe:

> Take off, take off those fine, fine clothes
> And lay them on this rock, *etc.*

The words and phrases used in narrating incidental details
reflect in general the pattern of conversation one finds among
rural folk in the American midregion. The following couplets
are from a version of "The Twa Sisters" (10) collected by
Brewster in Indiana:

> The youngest daughter she got her a beau,
> *etc., etc.,*
> The eldest daughter she had none.
>
> Her beau he got her a beaver hat,
> *etc., etc.,*
> The oldest daughter she didn't like that.

An example of this ballad found by Hudson in Oxford, Mississippi, narrates the same events with the same redundant
pronouns. Among other colloquialisms, the older daughter, who
hasn't received "a single thing," thinks "hard" of Johnny's
attentions to the younger sister:

> Johnny give the youngest a gay gold ring,
> He didn't give the oldest a single thing.
>
> Johnny give the youngest a beaver hat,
> The oldest she thought hard of that.

The miller was hung on the gallows so high,
The oldest she was buried close by.

The love scene in an example of "Young Beichan" (53) from Wisconsin (appearing under the title "Lord Baitman" in Arthur Beatty's collection) transpires with all the emotional fervor of modern true-romance fiction:

She led him down to the lower cellar
And drew him a drink of the strangest wine,
Saying, "Every moment seems like an hour,
Oh, Lord Baitman, if you were mine."[17]

Yet the lady is able to contain her passion for a good many moments and hours, seven years having "rolled around" when she decides to go look for Lord Baitman:

Seven long years have rolled around,
It seemed as if it were twenty-nine;
She bundled up her finest clothing,
And declared Lord Baitman she'd go find.

In an example of "Lord Thomas and Fair Annet" (73) collected in Kansas by Tolman the archaic word *riddle,* meaning *to counsel,* has been altered to its modern usage as a noun in one line, but retains its older verb usage in the next line, wherein the order is to "riddle it all in wool" (perhaps a corruption of "riddle it all in one" in Child's versions):

"Go read me a riddle, dear mother," said he,
"Go riddle it all in wool . . ."

An example of "Fair Margaret and Sweet William" (74) from Belden's Missouri collection speaks of sheets that "hang around" corpses:

"Fold back, fold back those flowing white sheets,
. . . . me now decline;
For today they hang around Lady Margaret's corpse
And tomorrow they shall hang around mine."

Another version of the same ballad, collected by Brewster in
Indiana, describes Lady Margaret's grief in casual language
lacking in emotional intensity:

> Lady Margaret threw down the ivory comb
> And vanished from that place,
> And all that day and all that night
> Lady Margaret was seen no more.

An example of "Barbara Allen" (84) found by Mabel Major
in East Texas is notable for the new tone assumed by the servant toward his master:

> He sent his servants to the town,
> And also one to her dwelling,
> Saying "Willie's sick and sent for you,
> If your name is Barbro Allen."[18]

This phrasing contrasts sharply with the deadly serious drama
of the Child versions; the manner in which the servant refers
to "Willie" and addresses "Barbro" Allen is outstanding for its
casualness, reflecting the relaxed relationship between servant
and master in the American setting. The final stanzas have
added details not found in Child's versions, particularly in the
description of the vines growing out of the lovers' graves:

> Sweet Willie was buried in the churchyard
> And Barbro buried beside him;
> Out of Willie's grave sprang a bright rose,
> And also one from Barbro's.
>
> They grew so high in the new churchyard,
> Why should they grow any higher?
> They looped, they tied in true love knots,
> They lived and died together.

The prize for understatement in narrative technique probably should go to Belden's example of "Little Musgrave and
Lady Barnard" (81) from Missouri, with its description of the
warning Little Mathy Groves's friend tries to send him on
his horn:

> There was one man among them all
> Who owed little Mathy some good will,
> And he put his bugle horn to his mouth
> And he blew both loud and shrill.

Several ballad narratives are open to infusion of religious or moral lessons, notably "Sir Hugh, or, The Jew's Daughter" (155) and "The Wife of Usher's Well" (79), as is seen in a stanza from an example of the latter found by Belden in Missouri:

> She prayed to God, if there be any God,
> If there be any God on high,
> To send her three little babes back home
> That night or soon next day.

In a version of the same ballad discovered by Louise Pound in Nebraska the parting of the babies from their mother has acquired a religious overtone. Instead of regretting that they must, as spirits, return to the grave before daylight, they express hope of a reunion in heaven:

> "A sad farewell, kind mother dear,
> We give the parting hand,
> To meet again on that fair shore
> In Canaan's happy land."

Tolman records an example of "Sir Hugh, or, The Jew's Daughter" in which the young boy calls for a prayer-book:

> If any of my playmates should call for me,
> You may tell them that I'm asleep;
> But if my mother should call for me,
> You may tell her that I am dead,
> And buried with a prayer-book at my feet.

Two examples of the same ballad collected by Randolph in the Ozarks repeat the young boy's request for the prayer-book, in one instance mainly for the sake of rhyme, apparently:

Oh, put the prayer-book at my head,
The Bible at my feet,
And when my playmates call for me,
Tell them that I'm asleep.

Oh, put the prayer-book at my feet,
The Bible at my head,
And when my parents call for me,
Tell them that their little one's dead.

This scene has been borrowed, with variations, by an example of "The Two Brothers" (49) found by Brewster in Indiana, not a surprising switch in view of the similarity of the death scenes in the two ballads:

Bury my Bible at my head,
My satchel at my feet,
My little bow and arrows at my side
When I am sound asleep.

The influence of oral tradition on some Child ballads in the midregion has become apparent in the garbling of names, phrases, and even whole stanzas as the narrative is transferred from one singer to another. For example, in Child's version *H* of "Lady Isabel and the Elf-Knight" (4) the murderer promises the girl they will go to "some unco' land," some unknown place to which they can flee with the gold, whereas some midregion versions (like this example collected by Belden in Missouri) change the destination to a meaningless phrase:

Hand me down your father's gold,
Likewise your mother's too,
Away we will go to the marigold country,
The length of a long summer day.

An example of the same ballad collected by Brewster in Indiana names another place, also unidentifiable:

And I'll take you to the bonny sea sands,
And then we'll marry at Dee, O Dee,
And then we'll marry at Dee.

Equally meaningless phrases have crept into other ballads of the region. In a version of "The Twa Sisters" (10) found by Earl J. Stout in Iowa, the older sister replies as follows to the pleas of the younger to be pulled out of the water:

> "I'll neither lend me my hand or glove,
> I'll be true, true to my love," *etc.*[19]

The words *lend me* might have resulted from an error in transcribing, or could represent alteration by oral tradition from *lend thee*—one of Belden's Missouri versions has it "I will neither lend you my hand nor glove." This same Missouri example, however, also embodies an equally unexplained term, *native land:*

> "Oh sister, O sister, lend me your hand
> To help me to the native land."

Not only are single names and phrases occasionally mispronounced and garbled, but whole scenes are sometimes confused, as in an example of "The Two Brothers" (49) collected by Hudson in Mississippi:

> Two little boys were going to school,
> They were playmates for to be;
> Willie said to Johnnie,
> "Can you throw a rock or toss a ball?"

The foregoing examples of unique vocabulary and phrasing have been the result of misinterpretations and mispronunciations of elements that belonged to the ballads before they entered the midregion. There are other unique terms, however, which have no antecedents among earlier versions; thus we can assume that the ballads acquired them from one of the speech areas of the region.

Charles Neely's example of "Fair Margaret and Sweet William" (74) from southern Illinois speaks of Lady Margaret's "grimly ghost." In an example of "Lord Thomas and Fair

Annet" (73) from the same collection Lord Thomas asks his
mother to "discourse" in place of the usual request to "riddle"
in solving his dilemma:

> "Oh, Mother, dear Mother, will you discourse,
> Will you discourse as one?
> O shall I marry fair Elender dear,
> Or bring the Brown girl home?"

In an example of "Lady Isabel and the Elf-Knight" (4) collected by Hudson in Mississippi, the lady pronounces the murderer a "rebel"—a possible reference to the Civil War, though
there are no other elements in this version that could be so
related:

> "O turn yourself around and about
> To view the leaves on the trees,
> For it don't become a rebel like you
> To watch a lady like me, me, me," *etc.*

In Hudson's "Earl Brand" (7) Fair Elinor "slipped on" her
clothes and informed Sweet William that he might be "mad
or pleased" as he wished—*mad* signifying *angry*:

> Fair Elinor arose, slipped on her clothes
> For to let Sweet William in,
> So ready was she to go with him
> And leave all the rest of her kin.
>
> "Be mad or pleased," Fair Elinor she said,
> "Be mad or pleased as you may be;
> I wish myself in old Ireland
> And you in the middle of the sea."

Hudson's example of "Young Hunting" (68) has the tone of the
Mississippi pine forest community in which it was collected:

> "He's been a-hunting these three long days,
> I expect him home tomorrow," *etc.*

In "The Maid Freed from the Gallows" (95), the instrument

of death is usually "the gallows tree." A version discovered by Hudson has substituted the term *sorrow tree*, which might be considered a decided improvement in poetic quality:

> "Father, O father, did you bring your gold?
> Did you come to buy me free?
> Or did you come to see me hung
> Along the sorrow tree?"

The word *biler* is used to describe Lord Thomas' occupation in an example of "Lord Thomas and Fair Annet" (73) collected by Albert Tolman in Kansas:

> Lord Thomas he was a bold biler, sir,
> A biler, sir, was he;
> Fair Elender being an accomplished young lady,
> Lord Thomas he loved her dearly, dearly,
> Lord Thomas he loved her dearly.

Many versions of this ballad describe Lord Thomas as "a forester and a chaser of the King's deer." Thus, the term *biler* could be related to *byrlawman*,[20] a minor rural officer in England, and would not be considered a local creation.

It was pointed out above that the verse pattern of midregion ballads is more flexible than that of the Child originals, often becoming so variable in meter as to present the appearance of conversation rather than poetry, while still adhering in general to the basic four-line ballad stanza made up of alternating lines of iambic tetrameter and iambic trimeter. An example of "James Harris (The Daemon Lover)" (243) from Brewster's Indiana collection begins with a stanzaic arrangement according to the regular pattern, but the first line of the fourth stanza then deviates drastically:

> She hadn't been on the sea more than two weeks,
> I'm sure it wasn't three,
> Till this fair damsel began to weep,
> And she wept most bitterly.

Stanza 5 of an example of "Young Hunting" (68) recorded by
Belden in Missouri possesses an unusual metrical arrangement
in that a word of primary importance, *live*, becomes an unaccented syllable in the iambic foot, disrupting the standard-form
rhythmic pattern set by preceding stanzas:

> "Live half an hour, Young Henry," she said,
> "Live half an hour for me,
> And all the men in our town
> Shall give relief to thee."

The following stanza from "Fair Margaret and Sweet William"
(74), discovered by Brewster in Indiana, also lacks regular
meter:

> The day being past and the night a-coming on,
> When most of the men were asleep,
> Lady Margaret came walking softly downstairs
> And stood at William's bed feet.

Such irregularities are even more noticeable when one encoun-
ters variable metrical patterns from one stanza to another, as
in a version of "Lady Isabel and the Elf-Knight" (4) collected
by Gardner and Chickering in Michigan. The first stanza is
made up predominantly of anapestic feet; the second is predominantly iambic. The third goes to anapestic again with an
extra unaccented syllable in the third line:

> There lived a false knight in London did dwell
> Who courted a lady fair;
> And all that he wanted of this pretty maid
> Was to take her life away.

> "Go get part of your father's gold
> And part of your mother's fee;
> And we will go to some strange country
> Where married we shall be."

> She went and got part of her father's gold
> And part of her mother's fee;
> O she went, O she went to her father's stable-door,
> Where the horses stood fifty by three.

The first, fourth, and eighth stanzas from a version of "James Harris (The Daemon Lover)" (243) found by Belden in Missouri display extreme variations which, although not typical of the entire midregion, are certainly to be found in more than one ballad:

> "We have met, we have met, we have met, my dear
> We have met, we have met," said he;
> "For I've just returned from the salt, salt sea,
> And 'twas all for the love of thee."
>
> "If you will forsake your house-carpenter
> And go along with me,
> I'll take you where the grass grows green
> On the banks of the sweet Dundee."
>
> "What are you weeping for? My gold?
> Or is it for my store?
> Or is it for your house-carpenter
> That you never expect to see any more?"

Additional flexibility of form in ballad verse can be seen in the less common variation of stanzas by number of lines. An example of "Sir Hugh, or, The Jew's Daughter" (155) recorded by Tolman in Indiana contains stanzas made up of five lines, the fifth line being a repetition of the fourth; but the final stanza alters this arrangement with the addition of a sort of afterthought:

> "If any of my playmates should call for me,
> You may tell them that I'm asleep;
> But if my mother should call for me,
> You may tell her that I am dead,
> And buried with a prayer-book at my feet,
> And a Bible at my head, head, head,
> And a Bible at my head."

Asher E. Treat's example of "James Harris (The Daemon Lover)" (243) collected in Wisconsin is made up mainly of four-line stanzas. In the fourth stanza, however, James Harris in promising the carpenter's wife a better life offers to take her

to the banks of not one but two streams, adding a fifth line to
the stanza:

> "If you'll forsake your house carpenter
> And go along with me,
> I will take you where the grass grows green,
> On the banks of the Sweet Willee,
> On the banks of the Sweet Liberty."[21]

In an example of "The Three Ravens" (26) discovered by
Earl J. Stout in Iowa, the ballad stanza is prolonged not by
variation of number of lines—the stanzaic arrangement is consistent—but by elaboration of the nonsense refrain, which is
characteristically interwoven with the narrative couplets:

> There were three crows sat on a tree,
> Oh Billy Magee Magar!
> There were three crows sat on a tree,
> Oh Billy Magee Magar!
> There were three crows sat on a tree,
> And they were black as crows could be,
> And they all flapped their wings and cried
> Caw, Caw, Caw, Billy Magee Magar!
> And they all flapped their wings and cried
> Billy Magee Magar!

4. *The Comic Treatment*

Child ballads developing comic situations are prominent in
the American midregion, as might be expected in view of the
area's general cultural characteristics. Among those found
retaining the comic strains of the originals, with added elements
in some versions, are "Our Goodman" (274), "The Wife Wrapt
in Wether's Skin" (277), and "The Farmer's Curst Wife" (278);
eight examples have been found of the first, nine of the second,
and ten of the third.

There is also, however, a noticeable tendency in the midregion to convert ballads of pure tragedy into mock-tragic nar-

ratives, with addition of comic overtones. The reasons behind such a tendency to make light of serious themes are not far to seek. In a dynamic social order such as that of the frontier, where all things are on the move and new institutions are barely established before they are changed to conform to the shifting social tide, one would expect to find a taste for narratives that describe action and accomplishment. One of the predominant characteristics of such a region's people would be their profound optimism, which would make them impatient with tragic failure, with tragedy for tragedy's sake. Ballads of work and occupation are in the ascendancy, as in Earl C. Beck's collection from northern Michigan, made up largely of work ballads of the lumberjack modeled upon the broadside style. Only one Child ballad was located by Beck, and that a comic one: "The Farmer's Curst Wife" (278). The folk of the American mid-region were inclined to treat lightly those ballads which did not reflect pride and accomplishment in one's occupation.

In its migration west of the Appalachians "The Elfin Knight" (2), as we have observed, loses its supernaturalism and becomes a ballad of courtship between two lovers. Some examples also develop a comic theme with the girl expressing amusement instead of fear as she sidesteps the old man's attentions, as in Belden's Missouri version:

> Are you a-going to Boston, sir?
> Just give my respects to an old man there.
>
> Tell the old fool, when he's done this work
> To bring me the land and I'll give him the shirt.

In an Indiana example found by Brewster, the courtship of two young lovers takes a humorous turn in the mutual assignment of tasks, presumably tests of affection:

> If you go up to town tonight,
> Just hand this note to that young miss,
>
> And tell her to make me a fine shirt,
> And make it out of an old cotton sheet.

If you go down to town tonight,
Just hand this note to that young gent.

And tell him to plow it with a ram's horn,
And seed it down with one grain of corn.

Tell him to reap it with his penknife,
And haul it in with two yoke of mice.

In examples of "Lady Isabel and the Elf-Knight" (4) found in the region, the manner in which the murderer approaches the lady in the beginning and her way of doing him in never maintain the basic seriousness of these scenes as presented in the Child collection. In a version reported by Belden from Missouri the murderer (identified as "Willie," a name most unlikely to be associated with mysterious evil-doers) is "dipped" in the sea:

Willie came over the main, wide ocean,
Willie came over the sea,
Willie came over the main, wide ocean,
Willie came courting me.

She turned her face to the green willow tree,
Her back to the bottom of the sea;
She gathered him around the slender waist
And dipped him into the sea.

In examples of "The Twa Sisters" (10) found in the mid-region the miller (or the miller's son), something of a hero in the Child versions, is frequently presented as a great fool or stupid villain, as in a humorously-toned version from Belden's Missouri collection:

Down she sank and away she swam
Until she came to a miller's mill-dam.

"Miller, O miller, lend me your hand,
And I'll give you a gold inkstand."

The miller accepted the golden inkstand
And then he pushed her in again.

The miller was hung on his mill-yard gate
For drownding of poor sister Kate.

The saddles and bridles are hanging on the shelf;
If you want any more you can sing it yourself.

An even more humorous approach to the same originally tragic
situation is reported by Gardner and Chickering in their collection of ballads from Michigan (though the version should
actually be assigned to Nebraska, home of the informant, who
was visiting in Michigan when interviewed there by the
collectors):

Peter and I went down the lane,
Down the lane, down the lane,
Peter and I went down the lane,
And sister came behind.

Both of us sisters loved him well,
Loved him well, *etc., etc.,*
As only I can tell.

Peter could love but one of us then,
So sister must go away.

Sister was bending over the well,
When splash, splash, in she fell.

Peter and I were wed one day,
And oh, what people did say!

Peter then left for foreign parts,
And I'll die of a broken heart.

In "Lord Randal" (12) the question-and-answer scene usually develops in an atmosphere of mounting suspense as the
mother begins to realize what has happened to her son. A lapse
into violent speech on the part of either character would immediately break the spell of the tense dramatic situation and
reduce it to seriocomic melodrama; yet just such a condition
exists in an example of the ballad collected by Tolman in
Indiana:

"Oh, what did you will to your sweetheart,
Johnnie Ramble my son?
Oh, what did you will to your sweetheart,
My own dear little one?"
"All hell and damnation for to parch her soul brown,
For she is the one that has caused me lie down."

An ancient ballad of great seriousness, "Sir Lionel" (18)
narrates the epic fight between a knight and a wild boar which
had killed many men. An example reported from Missouri by
Belden under the title "Bangum and the Boar" develops the
story with a strange blend of the comic and the serious. Sir
Lionel who in Child's version A "wold on huntynge ryde" has
become "Old Bangum" who "would a-wooing ride":

Old Bangum would a-wooing ride,
Dillum down, dillum down,
Old Bangum would a-wooing ride
Dillum down,
Old Bangum would a-wooing ride
With sword and buckler by his side,
Cum-e-caw, cud-e-down, kill-e-quo-qum.

The refrain is typical of the examples found in the midregion,
and here it emphasizes even more the nonserious tone of the
ballad in its opening lines. The introductory stanza is con-
structed much like that of "Mr. Frog Went A-Courtin'." In the
second stanza Bangum meets "a pretty maid," an additional
suggestion of the comic, since in Child's A she is presented as
"a lady" who is in trouble because her knight has been slain.
No mention is made of the slain knight in the Missouri example,
which up to this point sounds like a story of courtship between
an old man and a pretty girl. Subsequent stanzas, however,
develop the more serious aspects of Bangum's fight:

Old Bangum rode to the greenwood side,
And there a pretty maid he spied.

"There is a wild boar in this wood
That'll cut your throat and suck your blood."

"Oh, how can I this wild boar see?"
"Blow a blast and he'll come to thee."

Old Bangum clapped his horn to his mouth
And blew a blast both loud and stout.

The wild boar came in such a rage,
He made his way through oak and ash.

They fit three hours in the day,
At last the wild boar stole away.

Old Bangum rode to the wild boar's den,
And spied the bones of a thousand men.

The nonsense refrain ("Billy Magee Magar!") of the example of "The Three Ravens" (26) collected by Earl J. Stout in Iowa, noted earlier, assumes a major role in the ballad and serves to introduce a comic element in what is basically the tragedy of a slain knight left unburied on the battlefield:

Said one old crow unto his mate,
Billy Magee Magar, *etc.*
"What shall we do for grub to ate?"

"There lies a horse on yonder plain
Who's by some cruel butcher slain."

A version of the same ballad found by Hudson in Mississippi conveys even stronger suggestion of a comic question-and-answer session:

One old crow says to his mate,
"What'll we do for grub to eat?"

His mate replies, "In yonders lane
Lies an old gray horse, just lately slain.

"We'll seat ourselves on his back-bone
And pick his eyes out, one by one."

"Lord Thomas and Fair Annet" (73) usually announce themselves at each other's doors, in both British and American

versions of the ballad, in such terms as "tirled at the pin,"
"tingled at the ring," "jingled at the ring." An example reported
by Belden from Missouri, however, develops this scene in a
different and rather comical fashion:

> He rode and rode till he came to her door,
> He wrote a letter and handed it in;
> So who was there so ready as she
> To rise and welcome him in.
>
> She rode and she rode till she came to his door,
> She wrote a letter and handed it in;
> So who was there so ready as she
> To arise and welcome him in.

A version of this ballad found by Hudson in Mississippi cites
Lord Thomas' bravery in undertaking courtship of the queen's
daughter:

> Lord Thomas, Lord Thomas he was a brave man,
> He courted the queen's daughter,
> The queen only had but one only daughter,
> Fairrellater her name.

A prominent scene in many versions of "Fair Margaret and
Sweet William" (74) describes Lady Margaret's dramatic but
utterly calm decision to leave her bower and die, after she
spies Sweet William walking with his new bride (Child's
version A):

> Down she layd her ivory comb,
> And up she bound her hair;
> She went her way forth of her bower,
> But never more did come there.

An example from Belden's Missouri collection gives the scene
quite a different treatment, Lady Margaret being pictured as
a shrew who vows to go give Sweet William a piece of her
mind and then forget him. This ludicrous reversal of sentiment
is emphasized by a change of verb tense to the future, indi-

cating a rapidly rising anger and a conscious preparation for
venting it:

> "I'll throw down my ivory comb,
> I will just brush back my hair,
> And I'll go and make Sweet William bow,
> And no more shall I go back there."

Child's versions of "The Lass of Roch Royal" (76) relate a
long and tragic story of a maid turned away from her lover's
door, sent off with her child in her arms to die of grief. In contrast, all of the twenty-one examples of the ballad found in the
midregion omit the tragic events and reduce the narrative to
a flirtation between two lovers with repartee on the maid's
faithfulness while the young man is in a foreign land, as in this
version from Vance Randolph's Ozark collection:

> Oh who will shoe your pretty little feet,
> An' who will glove your hands?
> An' who will kiss your ruby, ruby lips
> When I'm in a furrint land?
>
> My father will shoe my pretty little feet,
> My mother will glove my hands,
> Nobody will kiss my ruby, ruby lips
> When you're in a furrint land.

Examples of "Barbara Allen" (84) found in the midregion
display changes from tragedy into comedy much like those seen
in the case of "Fair Margaret and Sweet William." In a version
of "Barbara Allen" recorded by Louise Pound in Nebraska the
usual somber tone shifts to one of light-hearted flippancy, in
a mockery of tragic death:

> Slowly, slowly she rose up,
> And to his bedside was going,
> She pulled the curtains to aside
> And said, "Young man, you're a-dying."

> He stretched out his pale white hand,
> Expecting to touch hers,
> She hopped and skipped all over the floor,
> And said, "Young man, I won't have ye."

The murder of Sir Hugh by the Jew's daughter is narrated in Child's version (155) with the seriousness of tone befitting a tragic situation. Examples of the ballad found in the mid-region, on the other hand, describe the knifing in language that conveys a sort of carnival atmosphere, the spirit of good times and feasting connected with the hog-killing season on a farm:

> She wrapped him in her apron
> And pinned it with a pin;
> She put him on her own bedside
> And stuck him like a pig.

This Indiana example recorded by Brewster manages a shift in tone from the tragic to the comic by changing one word: *pig* is substituted for *swine* in the Child original. In a version from Alabama presented by Louise Pound, Child's verb *stuck* is humorously modified to *stobbed:*

> She took me then by her lily-white hand,
> And led me in the kitchen,
> She laid me down on a golden plank,
> And stobbed me like a sheep.

"The Farmer's Curst Wife" (278) narrates a humorous situation in all versions, English and American. Examples found in the American midregion, where the ballad is especially popular, outdo the Child versions in description of the wife's shrewish character, as in the stanza recorded by Gardner and Chickering in Michigan wherein the devil has brought back the farmer's wife and says to him:

> "Farmer, O farmer, I'm sorry to tell
> That your old woman reigns bully of hell."

Such extravagant phraseology is apparently of American origin, for nothing like it appears in the Child versions of the ballad. In the same tone, in an example found by Belden in Missouri, is the husband's comment after the devil has returned his wife:

> "Now, old woman, on earth you must dwell;
> You are not fit for heaven, and they won't have you in hell."

5. Fragmentation

Another characteristic of Child ballads in the midregion is their general reduction in length, as evidenced both by shortening of narratives and by decrease in average number of stanzas. Collectors of the region also have reported discovery of numerous ballad fragments. Both factors suggest a tendency among the Child ballads of the midregion toward fragmentation.

So long as a ballad tells a complete story one would not ordinarily regard it as a fragment, even though it may omit episodes contained in an older version. Fragmentation occurs when the principal elements of a narrative are absent, regardless of the actual number of stanzas in the ballad. An informant will frequently report that the verses he furnishes are a fragment of a longer ballad that he once knew; on the other hand, he may sometimes compensate for forgetting part of one ballad by introducing an episode from another. Such migration of narrative elements is a normal characteristic of traditional literature, and the fact that the ballad in question has dropped a portion of its narrative in favor of a new episode does not make it a fragment. If, however, all the ballads within a certain region are greatly reduced in length in comparison with older versions, and if they consistently omit portions of narratives that are included in older ballads, then one might assume they have reached a point of stagnation and are moving as a mass toward fragmentation. Such a condition exists among the Child ballads of the midregion of the United States.

Table III below indicates the degree to which each of the forty-nine Child ballads found in the midregion has been reduced in length in its migration from England, as shown in average number of stanzas in examples found in the two places—with additional figures recording the number of fragments of thirty-four of the ballads discovered by midregion collectors. The over-all average length for all the Child versions listed is fifteen stanzas, as against seven for the same ballads as they exist in the midregion. It should be noted that the greatest reduction in length appears among ballads not well known in the midregion, where collectors have found only one example each of "Child Waters" (63), "Lizzie Lindsay" (226), and "The Suffolk Miracle" (272), ballads suffering reductions of twenty-six, twenty-one, and seventeen stanzas, respectively.

TABLE III

FRAGMENTATION OF CHILD BALLADS IN THE AMERICAN MIDREGION

Child No.	Title	CHILD Average No. of Stanzas	MIDREGION Average No. of Stanzas	Fragments Found
2	The Elfin Knight	13	9	1
3	The False Knight Upon the Road	9	4	
4	Lady Isabel and the Elf-Knight	17	10	7
7	Earl Brand	16	9	
8	Erlinton	22	7	1
10	The Twa Sisters	18	9	2
12	Lord Randal	8	5	5
13	Edward	10	6	1
18	Sir Lionel	21	4	2
20	The Cruel Mother	12	9	
26	The Three Ravens	8	4	10
46	Captain Wedderburn's Courtship	15	9	
49	The Two Brothers	16	7	
53	Young Beichan	31	10	1
54	The Cherry Tree Carol	13	2	1
63	Child Waters	29	3	1
68	Young Hunting	22	12	2
73	Lord Thomas and Fair Annet	28	14	9

Child No.	Title	CHILD Average No. of Stanzas	MIDREGION Average No. of Stanzas	Frag- ments Found
74	Fair Margaret and Sweet William	15	9	5
75	Lord Lovel	11	6	3
76	The Lass of Roch Royal	20	4	13
79	The Wife of Usher's Well	10	6	
81	Little Musgrave and Lady Barnard	25	8	3
84	Barbara Allen	11	9	9
85	Lady Alice	7	5	2
93	Lamkin	18	8	1
95	The Maid Freed from the Gallows	9	9	1
105	The Bailiff's Daughter of Islington	13	11	
112	The Baffled Knight	14	6	
155	Sir Hugh, or, The Jew's Daughter	11	5	3
173	Mary Hamilton	13	3	2
200	The Gypsy Laddie	12	7	5
209	Geordie	20	7	3
215	Rare Willie Drowned in Yarrow	11	7	
218	The False Lover Won Back	12	10	
226	Lizzie Lindsay	23	2	1
236	The Laird o' Drum	17	9	1
243	James Harris (The Daemon Lover)	17	11	2
250	Henry Martyn	8	12	1
272	The Suffolk Miracle	28	11	
274	Our Goodman	26	10	3
277	The Wife Wrapt in Wether's Skin	9	7	
278	The Farmer's Curst Wife	11	13	
279	The Jolly Beggar	20	3	1
286	The Golden Vanity	12	8	2
287	Captain Ward and the Rainbow	12	7	
289	The Mermaid	7	7	3
295	The Brown Girl	12	8	2
299	The Trooper and the Maid	10	6	
	Over-all Average:	15	7	

"Little Musgrave and Lady Barnard" (81), of which six examples have been located in the area, has lost seventeen stanzas on the average, while "Young Beichan" (53), with ten examples collected, has dropped twenty-one stanzas.

In the other direction, two ballads, "Henry Martyn" (250) and "The Farmer's Curst Wife" (278), gained in average num-

ber of stanzas in their migration to the midregion. The increase
for "The Farmer's Curst Wife" may be explained by its great
popularity as a humorous ballad; another of the same type,
"The Wife Wrapt in Wether's Skin" (277), averages only two
stanzas shorter in the midregion than in the Child collection.
The gain in average length shown by "Henry Martyn" may
come from the fact that four of the six examples collected in
the midregion contain narrative elements appearing in English
broadside versions of the ballad but excluded from Child versions, such as the quest for vengeance on the pirate Henry
carried out by Captain James Stuart and Henry's subsequent
hanging. The average for "Barbara Allen" (84) in the midregion is very close to that of the Child versions, attesting this
narrative's popularity as broadside material in both England
and America.

Additional evidence of the tendency toward fragmentation
is the large number of ballad fragments (109, of thirty-four
ballads) reported by collectors of the midregion. The number
is particularly impressive in view of the fact that not all collectors have followed the same practice in reporting fragments.
No comparative number of fragments of these ballads is found
either in the Child collection or among collections east of the
Appalachians.

1. MacEdward Leach, *The Ballad Book*, pp. 38-39.

2. William J. Entwistle, *European Balladry*, pp. 240-41.

3. Reed Smith, "The Traditional Ballad in America, 1933," *Journal of American Folklore*, XLVII, 73-75.

4. Helen Child Sargent and George Lyman Kittredge, editors, *English and Scottish Popular Ballads*, p. 91.

5. Paul G. Brewster, *Ballads and Songs of Indiana*, p. 57.

6. H. M. Belden, editor, *Ballads and Songs Collected by the Missouri Folk-Lore Society*, p. 34.

7. Louise Pound, *American Ballads and Songs*, p. 46.

8. Albert H. Tolman, "Some Songs Traditional in the United States," *Journal of American Folk Lore*, XXIX, 65.

9. A. P. Hudson, *Folksongs of Mississippi and Their Background*, p. 77.

10. Emelyn E. Gardner and Geraldine J. Chickering, *Ballads and Songs of Southern Michigan*, p. 48.

11. Charles Neely, *Tales and Songs of Southern Illinois*, p. 79.

12. Cecil J. Sharp, *English Folk Songs from the Southern Appalachians*, I, 7.

13. Phillips Barry, Fannie Hardy Eckstorm, and Mary Winslow Smyth, *British Ballads from Maine*, p. 26.

14. William A. Owens, *Texas Folk Songs*, p. 35.

15. Vance Randolph, *Ozark Folksongs*, I, 110.

16. Mary O. Eddy, *Ballads and Songs from Ohio*, p. 35.

17. Arthur Beatty, "Some Ballad Variants and Songs," *Journal of American Folk Lore*, XXII, 63.

18. Mabel Major, "British Ballads in Texas," *Tone the Bell Easy*, p. 148.

19. Earl J. Stout, *Folklore from Iowa*, p. 1.

20. *Byrlawman:* ". . . An officer appointed for various local duties. . . . arbitration in agricultural disputes, etc. . . . This still survives locally in Scotland and the north of England under various forms, . . . Burleyman, Birleyman, . . ."—*OED.*

21. Asher E. Treat, "Kentucky Folksong in Northern Wisconsin," *Journal of American Folklore*, LII, 46.

Six Tales from Mexico

RILEY AIKEN

El Que Canta Sus Males Espanta

THIS WAS A MAN who lived in the Kingdom of Ururú. By his friends he was called Chanito. And this name, it seems, came from Chano, and Chano from Borrachán, and Borrachán from the fact that he was a tippler.

Indeed, he wasted so much time and money in the bars he eventually found himself in the gutter with neither friends nor funds, and this hard circumstance forced him to conquer his bread on the highways and byways of the land.

And so it came about that upon one of so many, many days of wandering he met a man who, for a time at least, was destined to be his one and only friend. This *hombre* was a dealer in fine wines and he ran a cantina on the central plaza of the capital of the Kingdom of Ururú. But this one and only friend was no common cantinero with nothing more than a strong penchant for the almighty peso. He had a weakness for song, poetry, *la facilidad de la palabra*, and philosophy. Chanito appealed to his whims and intrigued him with such sayings as:

"Look, *amigo;* my vice, as you know, and I know and everyone knows is the *copa*, but in the game of life I am no rogue; I do not play with loaded dice," and "I like people who make a noise when they walk and sense when they talk; no rodeo, no subtle evasions, no traps."

One morning Chanito stopped at the cantina on the main plaza for conventional greetings and the customary *copita*. "*Quiubo*," he shouted, "*¿qué tal y cómo le amaneció?*"

There was no response. Toni, for this was the cantinero's name, sat behind the bar staring into space, a tragic picture of one who has been condemned, and executed, and is ready for the grave.

"*Oiga*, Toni," said Chanito, "first a drink and then out with the news. Tell me, have I pulled a *patraña?* What burdens your soul? Has someone done *mi amigo* something, perhaps? If I can help, I'm at your service. What's the trouble?"

"No, nothing is the matter," came a voice from the living dead. "It is only that I am to solve a riddle by tomorrow morning and if there is no solution I lose my hide."

"What hide, by the life of me! Is that all? Look, Toni, by the shades of all depths and little demons, don't be foolish. Riddles are child's play."

"Only this riddle is no child's play and it has no solution, Chanito," moaned Toni.

"*Bien, bien;* let's have a drink and then *manos a la obra*," said Chanito. "So little riddles we have, eh?"

"There is no use," said Toni. "Yet, if you insist, this is the way the cards are stacked. This morning while on my way to open my shop, Satan prompted me to sing a little song you taught me, and *peor que peor*, I was passing the palace gates as I sang it."

"So, what?" urged Chanito.

"In less time than it takes to say *santiamen*, I was arrested and taken before His Majesty, the King of the land."

"And charged with *lese magestad*, maybe?"

"No; accused of singing a song of propaganda, a song of reaction, that song of yours called 'Money Is All.'"

"*No le hace;* songs of reaction, flirtations with Her Royal Highness or stealing the King's ducks, the crime is *lese magestad*. And just for that you are to be skinned alive? *Mire, patrón*, the old law of tooth for a tooth fits this to a T. The King is foolish . . ."

"Sh . . ." warned Toni, "the walls have ears."

"What walls, what ears, and what lost *niño!* As I have said, the King is foolish. All royalty has one easy virtue. They pride themselves on their word, that is to say, a king's promise given. Surely he promised you something if you solve the riddle."

"Just my hide."

"Magnanimous of him, indeed. Well and good, we will play with His Majesty. We will stake our all on the Knave; that is to say on his weakness, his one convenient virtue, *'palabra del rey.'* But now, in order to help you I must know the nature and wording of the riddle."

"It is this, Chanito; tomorrow morning I am to tell him how much time and how much money will be required to teach a burro to read, and I am to perform the task myself."

"I presume His Highness is to provide the time and tuition," said Chanito. "We will take him at his word *'palabra del rey'* and we will say one thousand pesos in advance and one year." And then a shadow like a symptom of poison crossed the erstwhile jovial countenance of Chanito and he added with bitter sarcasm, *"Y con su pan se lo coma."*

"By my life, Chanito, no! Burros are burros. Who can teach a burro to read?"

"You, of course. Don't you remember? *Con el dinero todo se hace.* Ha, ha, *qué risa me da.* You yourself sang it. Perhaps you were not thinking. Perhaps you sang to cheer your heart and to frighten away some sad obsession. But such vague excuses would not hold before His Majesty's court. You and I will teach the burro to read and our *lema* will be *Keep your eye on the Knave,* and

> *No te aflojes,*
> *Ni te apoques."*

The next morning Toni went to the palace and gave his

answer and asked for the thousand pesos in advance—*palabra del rey*.

"One year, one thousand pesos and your burro will read?" asked the King.

"Yes, Your Majesty."

Toni and Chano bought a burro and for three days fed him nothing. They made a book of boards for leaves, and they covered the boards or leaves with symbols resembling the Chinese alphabet; and the leaves they hinged with rawhide. Then they put oats between the boards, and the burro soon learned to turn them to secure his food.

At the end of the year they took their educated ass to court and . . . What amazement! The animal turned the pages leaf by leaf, and finding nothing to eat brayed and brayed. And the people cheered and cheered.

"You win," said the King. "But this isn't all. I will give you a *plazo* of one day to tell me how long and how much money it will take to teach this animal to talk, and mind you, he is to talk a human tongue, and further there will be no advancement of funds."

Toni had no heart for more than one small question: *"Palabra del rey?"*

"Palabra del rey."

Chanito was waiting at the cantina when Toni came in. "What's wrong? You look worse than you did before. Didn't I warn you to watch for traps?"

"No traps, Chanito, just a new riddle, and this time if I fail to answer I am to be hanged. He demands now to know how long and how much money it will take to teach our burro to talk."

"Válgame Diós, Toni!" said Chanito. "And just for that you lose your stirrups? It is merely a matter of a new deal in which we substitute intestinal fortitude for heart, you remember the old saying, '*de tripas corazón,*' and if it comes to the worst, who cares? At birth a man is marked for death; we *are* today, and

tomorrow *away*. Ha, ha. A fig for death. Come, *amigo*, this is no time for worry."

"But what am I to do?" asked Toni.

"As we have done, Toni; as we have done. Remember, we stake all on the Knave as we did before, *palabra del rey*. Tell him, for a *plazo* of one hundred years and one million pesos we will teach our burro and a whole republic of burros to talk."

An argument followed, for Toni limped on the side of scruples. "An ass is an ass," he said. "Never can we teach this animal to talk."

"Listen, Toni; who cares? Don't you see? One hundred years from now the King, you, the burro, and the one who drives him will be at best a memory, *y nada más. ¿No le parece? No hay mal que cien años dura.*"

I had no time to listen further to this marvelous sense and nonsense, and I regret I do not know *a ciencia cierta* the end of the yarn. However, I do know that some days later I found Chano, alias Chanito, alias Borrachán just across the border from the wonderful Kingdom of Ururú, and he was all spider-foot with liquor, and he was staggering x's and s's with his legs, and was as happy as a loony lark, and he was singing:

> *De cuatro pares de pantilones*
> *No más me quedan los puros botones.*
>
> . . . . . .
>
> If more of this you wish to know
> Just go and ask the mamma crow,
> For some opine that it was she
> Who got this first from the ceiba tree.

Periquito, Wood Dealer

THIS IS A STORY about a parrot. And like most parrots, he saw too much, heard too much, and talked too much. However, this bird talked and talked until he, like some people, became presumptuous and proud. He was proud of his cap of gold and his green suit, proud of the purity of his speech, and proud of his place in society. Yet the thing that amused and annoyed the family with whom he lived was Perico's hatred for the cat and the dog. Nothing appealed more to his parrot sense of humor than to bite the tip of the kitty's tail and to sound false alarms by whistling to the dog. But the hateful pranks he played on the other pets and his love for languages have little to do with this story. Some day, if you will be good *niños*, I will tell you how he lost the feathers from his tail by mistaking a young leopard for a house cat; or how, another time, he talked himself into a job of teaching languages to other parrots.

But, as I have suggested, this story deals with presumption, and how he took it upon himself to purchase supplies for the family, and the price he paid for his error.

Well, the *señor, señora,* and the *niños* were away for the day and the cook was asleep when the vendor of stovewood came down the alley back of the house. He called: "*¡Leña, leña! ¿Quién quiere comprar leña? Leña, partida, leña partida-a-a.*"

Perico heard this and the devil prompted him to call out in the voice of his master: "*Dos cargas.*"

The *leñero* stopped his burros, and led two of them that were heavily packed with stovewood through the rear door of the large patio. He unloaded the wood, stacked it neatly in a corner as he had done so often before, and waited for the *señor* to pay the bill. Finally he said to himself, "*Mi patrón* is busy, no doubt. I shall return tomorrow for the money."

He led the two burros through the large door, closed it, and proceeded on down the alley with his *hatajo* shouting: "*¡Leña, leña-a-a!*"

The next day, before leaving town for the *monte*, he dropped by the place where he had left the two *cargas* of split wood to collect for it.

"What are you talking about?" asked the *patrón*. "You must be a bit *tomao*. I ordered no wood."

"O yes you did," said the *leñero*. "I was not in my cups when I entered town and I came down the alley and called, '*Leña, leña*,' as I have always done. And you answered, '*Dos cargas*,' as you have always done. By the mother of God I swear it."

"*Poco a poco*, Lencho," said the *patrón*. "I was out of town, my family was out of town. Only the cook was here, the cook and the dog, and the cat, and . . ."

And then an amused look mixed with resentment played about the eyes and lips of the *patrón*. "*Está bueno*, Lencho. There has been an error, but it will be all right. We can use the wood. Here is the money."

And then the *patrón* went about the house calling, "*Perico, periquito; ¿quiere nueces, periquito?*"

Presently he heard the parrot answer, "*Corra, corra*" (Run, run) which translated from parrot Spanish means, "Make it snappy."

Periquito got no nut and not even so much as a dry tortilla. He got instead the flogging of his life and only after he had bitten his *amo's* finger did he get away. He fled from the back porch into a bedroom and hid beneath the bed.

In the meantime the cook had surprised the cat stealing cream. Kitty too had got a flogging—a good one—and he too had hidden beneath the bed, and was there licking his wounds and trying to gather his wits when the parrot in a great hurry joined him. Now as I have said these two were not on speaking terms, but when Periquito saw the cat's bleeding ear, broken tail, and black eye, he became highly elated.

He laughed and said with affected sympathy, "*Oiga, carajo;* how many loads of wood did you order?"

No Pooch 'Em

AND THIS WAS A PARROT who talked too much. He was an old, old parrot that had been with the family for generations. You know, *patrón*, these birds, like elephants, are not plagued by time.

The *perico* of this story became more loquacious as the years went by and he developed such a disregard for the sensitivities of others that the children in the family wanted to know why he used words they were not permitted to use. The mother with much embarrassment explained, and failing to convince the *niños* went to the husband.

"Listen, Juan. This parrot is scandalous. The words he uses in the presence of the children and my friends are embarrassing, to say the least. And when he lets go a filthy word, he says it *a secas*, with not so much as *con su permiso*. We must get rid of him."

"I heard what you said at first, but I don't understand the last. Did you say 'get rid of him'? If you did the answer is *vete a pasear*, no, *a-qui*, and *no* in all the languages of Babel. Don't you realize what you are saying? Periquito is a member of the family, indeed more of a member than you or I. He belonged to *mi mamacita* and before that to *mi abuelita*."

"*Basta*," said the wife. "It's either Periquito or the family. Choose for yourself. Let me know before tomorrow." And out of the room she stormed.

At first Juan was only amused. "Her melodrama sins of overplay," he said. "She doesn't mean it." Then after that he became serious and went to the patio to take a siesta on a cot in the shade of a pomegranate tree.

His sleep was a half-sleep. He saw his wife riding a broom like an old witch and Periquito flying from room to room. His wife was swearing and Periquito, scandalized, was trying to cover his ears with his wings. And presently an owl said, "Halt, I have the answer."

Juan awoke. He sat as if entranced. "The owl," said he, "how in the name of Satan did he enter this crazy *maraña* of domestic troubles?"

And then his countenance began to glow like a *mañanita* in

August. He sprang to his feet and called, "María, María, I have the answer! The owl is the answer."

At lunch the cook had complained of an owl that had been eating the chickens. "We must kill the owl or build a chicken house," said she. "As long as these little animals roost in a tree it will be like in the story of the coyote and the *ranchero;* that is to say a chicken a day until all are gone."

"I have the answer!" shouted Juan to María, his wife. "We will take Periquito from his *percha con to-i cadenita.* We will chain his foot to a limb of the tree where the chickens roost. The owl will keep him awake all night and he will have to sleep by day. And *se acabó* with his swearing. Besides," he added, "maybe the talk of the *inocente* will frighten the owl away, and we will have more *pollo con arroz,* and the cook will be pleased, and you will be happy, and I can go about my business with no further bother."

María consented, for she was now ashamed of her tantrum and she could see in this arrangement an opportunity to save face.

Bueno, Periquito was chained to a limb of the tree on which the chickens were accustomed to roost. And that night came *Señor Tecolote,* saw the new chicken with a golden cap and green dress and lit on the limb beside him.

Well, you know *Patrón,* the habits of an owl are strange. They won't kill a chicken on the roost. Motivated by instinct or perhaps sportsmanship, they push the victim off the roost and catch it on the fly and away they go.

Bueno, the *Señor Tecolote* gave Periquito a slight push. Periquito was a bird of culture despite his profanity. He moved along the limb to give room to the stranger. The latter, however, pushed again.

"*Oiga, Señor,*" said Periquito, "*no me empuje.*"

"Who?" said the owl, and gave another push.

"*Pues no me empujes, amigo. ¿No ve usted que se me acaba la rama?*"

"Who?" said the owl and pushed again.

"This fellow," mused Periquito, "must be a *gringo* and can't understand."

Then resorting to Spanish, Kickapoo, parrot talk, and a lot of vulgarity he said in part—with *permiso de las señoras*—"*Tate quieta, gringo salado,* you [censored, and censored and censored again]—no pooch 'em! [don't push!]"

Juan Soldado

THIS FELLOW JUAN, after spending some time in the army, asked for his discharge. His final pay was eighteen pesos and eighteen centavos. He bought three *pedazos* of bread and took to the road in the direction of his *tierra*. Barely had he begun his hike for home when he encountered an old man seated beside the road.

"I am hungry," said he. "Give me, if nothing more, just a piece of bread."

Juan didn't know this man, but he was San Pablo. Juan gave him one of three pieces of bread he carried in his *mochila* and continued on his way.

Presently he met another old man who sat begging beside the road. This stranger was San Pedro. Juan grumbled an uncomplimentary word to himself about a republic of beggars, gave the *pordiosero*, or San Pedro, the second piece of bread, and passed by.

Farther up the road he met another beggar. This old man was God. Juan, not knowing God, became angry, but after a tirade of unspeakable words, he calmed down and gave away his last piece of bread. The old man smiled and said:

"I see you don't speak always from the heart. You are a good man and just for that I give you my blessings and of many *mercedes* I possess I shall give you one for the bread you gave me. What will it be? *Sea lo que fuere.*"

"Oh," said Juan, "I would like to believe that my knapsack has some magic power."

"Granted," said God. "Now when you need anything just say: '*Todo a mi mochila,*' and whatever you wish will enter your knapsack." They said goodbye.

Juan came to a small town and while on his way down a street he saw a large plate of sweet food in a window. He was hungry but did not care to spend the little money he had for sweets.

But then he thought of the old man's blessings. With a dubious grin he gave a command as if he were a sergeant: "*Todo a mi mochila.*" Immediately the plate of sweet food disappeared from the window, and his pack seemed to grow heavier.

At nightfall he came to a town and asked for a place to sleep. There was no hotel, no inn, no place at all where a stranger could spend the night. Finally he found an old, abandoned house, but as he entered a man advised that he sleep elsewhere, that the place was the abode of ghosts.

"Everyone who sleeps there," said the stranger, "wakes up dead."

But this fellow Juan was a man of much valor and he entered the house and made his preparations to spend the night there.

About midnight he heard the rattle of small stones on the roof. He was unable to sleep and eventually he heard voices. They chanted: "*Caigo, o no caigo; caigo, o no caigo.*"

"*¡Caigan!*" said Juan.

The chanting ceased and Juan saw a legion of devils standing before him.

"*Todos a mi mochila,*" he ordered. And they entered his knapsack.

Juan is rich now. He uses these devils in his financial dealings. But every night before going to bed he puts his money in a bank.

La Cenicienta Huasteca

MARÍA LA CENICIENTA was a girl who worked for a woman
who had a daughter. She had to do all the housework and
besides was compelled to labor at night carding wool. However, there was a little lamb that helped her. And this story
tells us that the woman learned about this and ordered the
lamb killed. Also she called this girl, La Cenicienta, and told
her to take the stomach of the lamb to the river and wash it
and prepare it for *menudo*. While she was at the river preparing the meat for *menudo* some fish came and carried the little
stomach away. La Cenicienta began to cry.

Then a fairy woman told her to weep no more, that near by
was a small house and in the house was a baby crying and some
large *tinajas* (ollas) turned upside down.

"Sing to the baby and put it to sleep," she said; "then turn
the *tinajas* upright."

La Cenicienta did as that fairy woman ordered. She found
the small house and the baby crying. She sang and the little
one went to sleep. Then she turned a *tinaja* upright and immediately a golden star fixed itself upon her forehead and she was
dressed in fine clothes. She turned another *tinaja* and there
found the *menudo* meat prepared for cooking.

When she returned home the woman and the girl wanted
to know how she got the fine clothes and the star. La Cenicienta
told them what had happened at the river.

Envy entered the hearts of the woman and the girl and
they took the clothes from her. Then the woman had another
lamb killed and sent her daughter to the river with the stomach
of the animal.

"Do as La Cenicienta did," she said. "You will get more
beautiful things."

The daughter took the meat to the river and while washing
it some fish came and carried the little stomach away. Then the
girl pretended to weep. A fairy woman came to her and said:

"Weep no more. Go to the little house near here. You will find a baby crying. Sing it to sleep. Then the *tinajas* you see in the house are to be turned upright."

That girl went to the small house and she whipped the baby hard. She turned a *tinaja* and the *moco* of a *guajolote* attached itself to her forehead. She went home and wrapped a cloth about her head to hide the *moco*.

Later, the woman and her daughter went to mass. La Cenicienta was in the kitchen weeping and working when a fairy woman came to her and asked why she was sad.

"I wanted to go to mass," said La Cenicienta, "but they wouldn't let me." And then the fairy woman gave her a wand of *visfud*. "When you wish with your heart for something that is good, touch the star on your forehead with this wand and your wish will come true," she said.

Immediately La Cenicienta wished for elegant clothes and golden shoes and a carriage *mejor que ninguno* with a span of fine horses.

She went to mass and everyone was amazed and a prince fell in love with her.

When later the woman and her daughter came home they found La Cenicienta in her ashy clothes working in the kitchen. They told of the miracle that they had seen at mass.

"The miracle was I," said La Cenicienta.

They laughed and mocked and said the star on La Cenicienta's forehead was taking the salt from her brain.

The following Sunday the woman and daughter went to mass, and as before left La Cenicienta home. However, this time La Cenicienta did not weep. She used her wand of *visfud* as she had done before and behold she was at mass as beautiful as the most beautiful fairy.

When La Cenicienta left the church she lost one of her golden shoes near the door. The prince found it and went to the home where the woman lived with her daughter. He said he intended to marry the girl whose foot would fit that shoe.

The woman's daughter crammed her big foot into the shoe. The prince put her in his carriage and was on his way to his palace when a little dog began barking and saying: "*Moco de guajolote iba en coche y estrella de oro estaba en casa.*" The prince was puzzled and went back to the house where the woman lived. He found the beautiful servant La Cenicienta. The golden shoe fitted her foot. They were married, *y fueron muy felices.*

Juan de Toluca

THE KING AND THE QUEEN had been married thirty years and they had had no children at all, not one. One day the Queen told the King that she was going to have a baby and that it was her wish that it be baptized by a little old man who lived out in the mountains, a woodcutter. And the King said that he had no objections to this.

The following day the King sent some troops to open a road into those mountains so that he could go in person to invite the woodcutter and his wife to the baptism. And when the road was finished the King took a buckboard and went to the place where the little old people lived.

When the King invited them they asked if it were true that they were to have such a great honor as that of being god-parents with the King. And the latter said that it was true indeed. Then the little old man said that if this be the desire of Their Majesties he and his wife would accept. Then the King departed.

The next day the King sent some servants with clothing and provisions and with orders that the little old people be fed and bathed and properly clothed.

One week later the child was born and the King went to the mountains and returned with the little old people.

At birth the child had teeth and could talk. The little old people entered the King's house to congratulate the Queen.

And then they went to see the baby and the baby greeted them.
They were amazed and said:

"*Comadre,* the child has teeth and can speak."

And then the baby said to the Queen:

"Have them give my *tata padrino* a purse of *reales* to be
scattered among the poor on the way to the baptism."

After the baptism the King gave a banquet that lasted eight
days. And then the little old man told the King that he could
not be away from his home *tanto día,* that his house had no one
to look after it. Then the baby told the King to send servants to
care for the house until *tata padrino* could return home.

After the eight days of banqueting the baby said to the
King:

"Give my *tata padrino* two bags of *reales* so he won't have
to work as a woodcutter."

The little old people returned to their home in the mountains and the *viejito* said to his wife:

"All the same I am a worker; I must cut wood."

The following day he went to the *monte* and didn't return
until late at night. And then the woman said:

"Where is the wood you went to get?"

"I cut no wood. I spent the day catching this lion cub I
have here."

And then the little old lady said:

"What do you want with that animal?"

The *viejito* answered: "I want to take him as a gift to my
godson. This will be something he can play with."

And the little old woman said: "Yes, and that lion will eat
our godson."

The following day the *viejito* loaded on a small wagon
what wood he had about the place and went to the city. He
greeted the King and the Queen and his godson, and said his
only purpose in the city was to present a small lion cub to
his godson.

The present was accepted, and since the child was small

and the lion was small the Queen ordered a servant girl to keep
the lion near the cradle so that the two would become accustomed to each other.

The pet and the little prince grew as the months went
by and they learned to play together and to understand one
another. The lion never abandoned the boy.

One day the King asked the Queen:

"How are we going to separate the two? The lion is getting
large and some day he is likely to harm the child. I'm afraid
we will have to kill the animal."

The lion heard this and since he was a Prince that had been
enchanted years ago along with three cities, he understood
what was said.

"I am leaving," he said to the boy. "The King wants to
kill me so that you will be alone."

"If you go," said the boy, "I am going with you."

That night they ran away and took to a large range of
mountains. The lion provided the boy with food and water and
watched over his sleep to protect him from wild beasts.

Within fifteen days they had crossed the mountain range
and had come to a large sea. Then the lion said to the boy:

"Look; at this place you are going to mount on my back
and we will cross this sea."

They crossed to the other shore and continued to travel.

Then the lion said:

"Now I am going to put a legend on your forehead that
will read: 'I am Juan de Toluca.' Then you will change suddenly
from a little boy to manhood. And then you are to enter that
city yonder in the sunset's gloaming. A King who has three
daughters lives there and on the door of the castle there is a
sign that says: 'To that one who can cause the dead vines in my
vineyard to bear fruit again will be given one of my three
daughters in marriage.' Go into the city, find the palace, knock
at the door, and tell the King that you will cause the dead
vines to bear fruit again."

The next day the boy went to the King's house and knocked at the door. The King came out and said:

"What are you doing around here, Juan de Toluca?"

And the boy said: "I was on my way by when I saw this sign on your door and I have decided to make your vines green up and bear fruit again."

"Come in," said the King.

"I did not come to visit," said Juan. "*Yo, a lo que vengo, vengo*. Tomorrow have ready a hoe, a spade, and a bucket. Goodbye."

With no more magic than hard work and water, Juan caused the vines to green up and produce. He borrowed a basket and pan from the King and soon returned with fruit of many varieties.

"Come in, Juan de Toluca," said the King.

"I did not come to visit," said Juan. "*Yo, a lo que vengo, vengo*. Now I want your youngest daughter." After considerable haggling the King agreed to the demand. The Princess and Juan were married and went immediately to the mountains. There he found a castle instead of a cave.

"How did this happen?" asked Juan.

"*Son cosas mías*," was the lion's answer.

The two older daughters of the King ordered spies to follow Juan and their sister. These spies found the castle in the mountains and directed the sisters to it. They were amazed at the wealth and beauty of the place and when they returned home they told their father the King all about it.

"Fine," said the King, "now that I have a war on my hands with the Moors I will have Juan lead my army. He will be killed, my army will whip the enemy, and we will get the castle in the mountains."

After arrangements were made for Juan to lead the King's armies, the lion called him aside and said:

"Let the army precede you. After the forces are gone then I shall change into a poor horse, you mount me, and I shall take you beyond the black lagoon. When I jump in you are not to fall off. On the other side you are to kill all the Moors *a puros machetazos;* then the war will be over."

When Juan reached the field of battle he found the King's forces in flight. He killed all the Moors and returned to the mountains on his poor horse.

The King, upon learning what had happened, said:

"We will try another scheme to rid ourselves of Juan. Tomorrow there will be a *corrida de toros.* One of the three bulls will surely kill him."

The lion heard of this, went to Juan, and said:

"Juan, tomorrow you are to be a bullfighter. The three bulls are enchanted cities. You are to kill them. This once accomplished, the people will be free again and I shall regain my form as Prince. You are to keep one of the cities; the second will belong to me; and the third is to be governed by your *tata padrino* for his part in my disenchantment."

The bulls were killed and three *mesas* became three cities, ruled by the lion now a Prince, Juan de Toluca and his Queen, and his *tata padrino.*

The Western Bad Man as Hero

MODY C. BOATRIGHT

Look at the paperbacked Westerns on any newsstand, read the movie announcements in any daily, and you will meet the outlaw hero. The time will be between the Civil War and 1900, the locale will be west of the Mississippi, and the men will be mounted on horses and armed with six-shooters. The hero may or may not have a historic name, but whether he is called Jesse James or Alkali Ike, he is derived from a tradition which had its origin during the aftermath of the Civil War and which elevated some but not all the notorious desperadoes of the Southwest to the status of folk heroes.

These men became subjects of ballad, legend, and myth— prototypes of fictional characters exploited by writers for popular magazines, motion pictures, radio, and television. I am here concerned with myth, and only incidentally with fact. This concern, however, does not limit my sources to folklore and the products of the media of mass communication. Biography is also a fertile source of myth, especially the work of a biographer whose chief reliance has been upon the oral testimony of Jesse James's friends and relatives, or of one who records lengthy conversations that he never heard and puts down on paper exactly what Bob Ollinger was thinking at the very moment Billy the Kid shot him dead. For this investigation such writing is more significant than fact, for it is concerned not with what the bad man was like, but with what must be believed about him as a condition of his becoming a folk hero.

It is well to note that the bad-man hero flourished within a relatively short period of our history—from bleeding Kansas through the aftermath of Reconstruction. Of course we had our quota of lawlessness before and after, but the river pirates and slave stealers of the earlier time did not qualify as folk heroes; nor did the bootleggers and gangsters of a later period, despite a brief glorification in the pre-Will Hays movies. It is not, I believe, a historical accident that the bad-man hero attained his status in a culture pre-eminently dependent upon the horse. In the parent culture Robin Hood moved through Sherwood Forest on his own feet and proved himself a match for mounted men, but in America where the use of horses was not the prerogative of an aristocracy, I know of no counterpart who was not mounted on a swift and tireless horse.

In horsemanship, however, the bad-man hero did not differ essentially from his contemporaries.

Neither did he in origin. For the first requirement is that he belong to the dominant Anglo-American majority. Indians and half-breeds and Latins are excluded. A Joaquín Murieta might become a hero to the Latin-American in California and elsewhere, and even to Joaquín Miller, who appropriated his name; but never to a considerable number of Argonauts or their descendants. The chief repository of Murieta saga and myth is Chile.

The American bad-man hero must come, too, from the proper segment of the dominant majority—that is, from a respectable but not wealthy family. John Wesley Hardin and the James brothers were the sons of ministers. The Younger brothers were descended on their mother's side from Light-horse Harry Lee. Their father was a judge and sometime member of the legislature in Kentucky. A case is harder to make for Billy the Kid, who probably knew nothing about his father, not even how to spell his name. One story, more flattering to the mother than to the father, is that the latter met a young beauty of French extraction in New Orleans, followed her to Mississippi, and induced her to elope with him to New York, where he left her without carrying out his promise of marriage. Another is that the father was an Irish yeoman, that his landlord seduced and ruined two of his sisters, and that when he remonstrated he was thrown in jail on false charges, but managed to send his wife and young son to America. Billy always maintained that his mother was a lady, which in the New Mexico of the 1870's meant a woman of virtue. The fact that she ran a boarding house in Silver City in no way militated against her respectability.

A second requirement for admission to the rank of bad-man hero is an unfortunate childhood. Sometimes, like Billy the Kid, the hero has grown up in a rough mining town with no father to guide him. The James brothers lost their father early; they did not get along well with their first stepfather, Simms, though they loved their second, Dr. Samuel. They might have had a happy, normal youth had not the family been impoverished and persecuted by the depredations of the Jayhawkers, as were their relatives, the Youngers.

The youth from a respectable but unfortunate family, the pattern stipulates, commits his first crime under extreme provocation. Sometimes, as in the case of John Wesley Hardin, he is being abused by a freedman under the protection of the Yankees. Hardin went home and got the family six-shooter and killed the Negro. Some make this also the first crime of Billy the Kid. Others prefer to believe that his first victim was a man who insulted his mother; still others that the man was a married miner, who ran off with the Kid's fifteen-year-old sister. Dr. Samuel, the beloved stepfather of Frank and Jesse James, was peacefully plowing his field when the Redlegs seized him and hanged him to a tree. Jesse witnessed the deed, and after he and his mother had cut Samuel down and resuscitated him, Jesse rode away to join Quantrill.

Quantrill himself, according to his own accounts, had been

a peaceful and harmless schoolteacher until the Jayhawkers killed his brother. One Irvine Wally, a Federal captain whose soldiers had murdered her father, made unsuccessful love to one of the Younger girls. The man was married and his intentions were not honorable, and he blamed Cole for frustrating his attempt at seduction. He began to harry the youth, calling him a Quantrill man, thus making him one.

A fourth requirement is that the bad-man hero fight the enemies of the people. This does not mean that the people wholly approve the methods of warfare. In war, hot or cold, one must not scrutinize too carefully the morality of one's allies. The hero arises in a time of social conflict, and of course one's final estimate will depend upon one's sympathies in that conflict. Ask a New Mexican about Billy the Kid and his answer will depend in part upon the side his grandfather took in the Lincoln County War. Others know that the Kid fought the enemies of the small people called cattle barons, some of whom were thieves and murderers.

The Jameses, the Youngers, the Daltons, and their confederates fought first the Yankees, then those instruments of Yankee exploitation, the railroads, the express companies, and the banks. In an era of populism and rising progressivism they fought corporations as a matter of principle. Unfortunately their methods made necessary the deaths of a few servants of business; and they sometimes relieved innocent railroad passengers of their money and watches, but this was incidental.

Excluded from hero worship were the sellers of gun service to the rich—people like Tom Horn, gunman for big Wyoming cattle raisers, and Jim Courtwright, gunman for some of the southwestern railroads. And I am told by people who know that to this day a Pinkerton man cannot be the hero even of a detective novel. Feudists, however brave, cannot qualify. The Tewkesburies fought the Grahams; the Suttons fought the Taylors. Their quarrels were clannish and not in the public interest. The hero must in some sense be a public benefactor.

A fifth requirement is that during his career of outlawry, the hero perform acts of tenderness and generosity. Jesse James's family life was exemplary. His brother Frank enjoyed reading the classics, particularly the Bible and Shakespeare. One woman reports that Billy the Kid asked to hold her baby. He handled it tenderly and made much over it.

With tenderness went generosity. The outlaw hero robs the rich and gives to the poor. An old blind prospector called Mac Smith took pneumonia. Billy the Kid nursed him back to health and then put a rope in his hand. On the other end was a pack mule loaded with all the provisions a prospector needs. A play shows Billy giving $120 to a guitar player for medical aid for his sister. In the same play a deputy sheriff arrests a boy on false charges and takes his money. Billy makes him give it back. The deputy later makes the fatal mistake of drawing his gun. In one of the many movies about the Kid, the villain is the town doctor, who takes his fees in mortgages in lieu of money, then mercilessly forecloses upon the poor. Billy takes care of him.

Jesse James held up a stagecoach between Austin and San Antonio. Among the victims was a one-armed man. In response to Jesse's question he said he had lost his arm fighting for the Confederacy. Jesse gave him his money back. Once on a train Jesse robbed there was a sobbing woman. In the baggage car, she said, was the corpse of her husband. Jesse returned the $70 he had taken from her and added $120 as a gift.

A classic James story concerns another widow. After a successful robbery, Jesse and his gang were hiding in the bushes. They had been all day without food, and at dark they ventured to a farmhouse. A woman greeted them and agreed to cook them some supper. Her sorrow was apparent, and questioning revealed that the village Scrooge was coming with the sheriff that night to foreclose and dispossess her. The amount owed was $700. After the meal Jesse counted this sum out in currency, and told the woman to be sure when she paid the banker to have him sign a release and to have the sheriff witness his signature. Jesse and his men left, and before the banker got back to town after collecting from the widow, he was relieved of the money by the waiting outlaws. Robertus Love, who had this story from Frank James, accepts its authenticity, although it had earlier been told about Butch Cassidy. A recent movie gave the tale wide currency.

The outlaw hero must, of course, atone for his misdeeds. For the lesser ones like Frank James and Emmett Dalton a penitentiary sentence followed by a quiet, law-abiding life is sufficient. In fiction and drama the hero more often pays his debt by a change of heart manifested by his bringing to justice worse criminals than himself. Typical of the pulp fiction is a story in *Star Western* in which the outlaw saves a Ranger from being dragged to death by a wild steer to which two rustlers had tied him. He finds it good to be on the side of right, and on that side he remains. In a story by Gene Rhodes the outlaw Doolin has come to a town to case the bank. Some local men, hearing that Doolin is in the country, plan to rob the bank and pin the crime on him. He joins the good men and they capture the robbers, who turn out to be prominent and respected businessmen.

But in no case can the bad man attain redemption by turning informer against his associates. If the Whittaker Chamberses and the Herbert Philbricks of this age are heroes, something new has been added to the American tradition.

In biography, where a happy ending is less imperative than in popular fiction, the outlaw can attain the highest heroic stature only by an atoning death. That death must be a result of treachery and must have in it an element of martyrdom.

Sam Bass was betrayed by a comrade, Jim Murphy, bitterly denounced by the balladist:

> Jim had borrowed Sam's gold and didn't want to pay;
> The only shot he saw was to give poor Sam away.
> He sold out Sam and Barnes and left their friends to mourn—
> Oh, what a scorching he will get when Gabriel blows his horn.
>
> . . . .
>
> Perhaps he's got to heaven, there's none of us can say,
> But if I'm right in my surmise he's gone the other way.

Jesse James was shot in the back in his own house by a comrade seeking a reward:

> It was Robert Ford, that dirty little coward;
> I wonder how he does feel,
> For he ate of Jesse's bread and he slept in Jesse's bed,
> Then laid poor Jesse in his grave.
>
> . . . .
>
> The people held their breath when they heard of Jesse's death,
> And wondered how he ever came to die.
> It was one of the gang called little Robert Ford:
> He shot poor Jesse on the sly.

The man who told John Poe to look for Billy the Kid in Fort Sumner received not thirty pieces of silver, but one—a single silver dollar. Pat Garrett lay in ambush and shot Billy in a darkened room. Moreover, he baited the trap with a woman—whether Pete Maxwell's daughter or a servant girl is not determined.

The lives of most outlaw heroes end at death, but a favored few, notably Jesse James and Billy the Kid, live on. It is discovered years later that a substitute has been buried and the hero is now living an exemplary but obscure life. In 1950 Frank Dalton attained a brief notoriety by claiming to be Jesse James. His followers organized a Jesse James Society and attempted to establish his identity in court. His story was less plausible, however, than one that had circulated some forty years earlier. A respected banker and public-spirited citizen named Henry Ford died at Brownwood, Texas, and it was reported that Frank James was seen at the funeral. It later appeared that somebody had marked out *Henry Ford* and had written *Jesse James* on the tombstone, and many gave the bank robber credit for the banker's benefactions.

A half-dozen or more articles and stories have been concerned with the post-mortem life of Billy the Kid. The writer of one of these typically has met somebody who knows somebody who knows where the Kid is living. Marvin Hunter, for example, was told in 1899 that the Kid had not been killed at all. His sweetheart had persuaded Garrett to let him go. The Kid changed his name, went off to school either at Hico or Thorpe Springs, Texas, and became a respected and prosperous citizen.

Frank Dobie heard another story. He was in Magdalena, New Mexico, in 1937 when word was brought that Walk-along Smith's body had been found, out from Lordsburg. Walk-along had spent much of his time compiling information on the Lost Adams gold mine. He was often seen poring over the records in the archives of the Old Governor's Mansion in Santa Fe. When he died, Dobie writes,

> Then something of the enigma of this queer character's life was revealed—for some people. Walk-along Smith was Billy the Kid. The Kid . . . was not killed by Sheriff Pat Garrett. What was buried at old Fort Sumner was two bags of sand. Sheriff Pat Garrett and Governor Lew Wallace, realizing the character back of Billy the Kid's outlawry, sent him off to a far-away school. Years later he returned to New Mexico, a quiet, penitent, charitable man, who would not kill even a rattlesnake and was bent on living only the life contemplative. And eventually he was going to deliver the Adams Diggings to the cause of charity. Billy the Kid's ghost has walked in many forms.

All of which may testify to the American faith in education.

The bad-man myth is of course shaped in part by apologists, sometimes of doubtful veracity; in part by journalists seeking salable copy; in part by obscure and lonely persons seeking a moment's publicity; and in part by writers, often frankly fictionists, for the mass media, through which the myth is internationally disseminated.

Speculation as to why the myth takes this form rather than some other, to what extent it is national and to what universal, might well follow. At any rate it is a pattern imposed by the popular mind—that is, the mind of the American middle class—upon a prototypical historical character in order to make his career emotionally intelligible in terms of American culture. This mind sees no problem in a character almost wholly evil; it accepts the villain. It sees no problem, either, in a character in the main good. But a character who commits offenses against life and property, two things sacred in our culture, and who yet manifests traits of goodness, seems to require explanation. This simplified explanation is the myth of the western bad man.

Animal Tails: Function and Folklore

ROY BEDICHEK

IN THESE FEW PAGES of only so many words each I cannot permit my little assortment of tails, function and folklore, the fantastic liberties Nature allows, nor indulge the discursiveness of the folk imagination when it gets a good firm tail-hold. I see that I must bob even the few tails I have chosen for presentation here; or, as Caverley says, "curtail the already curtailed cur."

Near midnight some years ago I was lying abed with a book in a ramshackle camp house when I espied an enormous rat starting down a window casing headfirst. As I spotlighted him he stopped stone-still, and we regarded each other intently for several minutes. I was astonished that he could thus stay put on a fairly smooth perpendicular surface. By a stratagem I shall not take time to relate, I caught this rat. Lying in an unnatural hump, he measured sixteen and a half inches, half body, half tail.

I found the tail to be a scaly, cordlike organ, at the root about the size of my forefinger, tapering to about a tenth of that diameter at the tip. Fingering the powerful musculature about the root of this rat's tail and noting its rough, scaly surface, I became convinced that one of its functions is to assist feet and claws in maintaining the stability of the body, sitting, climbing, or descending. From that I went on trying to find other uses of the rat's tail, or reputed uses, the results

of which research were set forth in an essay incorporated in a
Texas Folklore Society publication a few years ago.[1] And, by
the way, one use I inadvertently omitted from that article
concerns the way papa and mama rats carry their newly born
babies by their tails. Now I find a pair of wretched laboratory
researchers scissoring off the tails of babies, generation after
generation, just to discover whether the rat learns to carry his
young by first holding the babe's tail in his mouth or whether
the act is inherited.

Coincidentally with my pursuit of the rat's tail, I found
other interesting tails, and discovered Nature to be devilishly
ingenious in her uses of them as well as quite relentless in
throwing them into the evolutionary ashcan. Nature not only
creates but is ever at work busily adapting organs to meet
new environmental conditions. She abhors not only a vacuum
but any organ without a function or one not fully utilized.
When she can find no further use for an organ, it is quietly
put away or, occasionally, accepted for a "bit part" or minor
role. Consider, for example, the prairie dog's tail, a mean survival of a once luxurious member, now serving merely as one
peg of the tripod which enables the rodent to sit upright, to use
his forefeet as hands to feed his face with, while still casting a
sharp eye over level distances for hawk or coyote. Just think
what has happened to this glorious tail since its owner descended from the trees and took to the open country! There are,
as we should certainly know, mammals with mere vestigial tails
tucked away under hair or even under the skin.

It seems to me that on no other external organ has Nature
worked more ingeniously and to better purpose than upon the
tails of rodents. Take for instance, the tail of the cute little
kangaroo rat—who, by the way, is neither a kangaroo nor a rat.
This particular sprig from a tiny branch of the great order of
Rodentia got lost in the wastelands of North America ages and
ages ago. Originally, it had the simple, serviceable little tail
of a mouse. But, stranded in the vast spaces of American

deserts, this mouselike little fellow couldn't make a living at night. He had to give up to a certain extent his nocturnal habits and often enough expose himself in broad daylight to such dangers as coyotes, snakes, cats, and hawks. Besides, food-producing areas were few and far between, so he had to become somewhat of a roamer and get out of reach of protective cover. Hence, Nature put into his hind legs a powerful spring which sends the little creature hurtling through the air eight or ten feet at one jump.[2] But a straightforward jump of that violence tended to tumble him over and over as he landed, so that the danger of his getting caught was increased. Apparently aware of the hazard, the Great Mother supplied him with a braking device, which took the form of an elongated tail finished off with a brush or banner at the end. So now when to avoid capture the kangaroo rat leaps high in the air some twenty times his body-length, he so manipulates the elongated tail as to zigzag himself to an unpredictable destination. Or he may use it to stop short, or to land with his head around the other way so as to be set for quick backtracking. He becomes an expert aerial dodger able to give his jump such an erratic course as often to frustrate his most agile and resourceful pursuers. Thus equipped, the kangaroo rat lives prosperously in our American deserts, multiplying up to a population in some areas of a thousand individuals to the square mile, while producing numerous genetic lines. A hundred different kinds of this charming little animal have been identified.

Now step, or jump, or vault (if imagination permits) from this creature of six-inch body-length to one standing flatfooted nineteen feet high: that is, to a mature bull giraffe. Here, to meet changing environmental conditions, Nature refashions both ends of an animal as essentially one project—neck and tail, while at the same time adjusting the forelegs for wider spread to permit grazing as well as browsing. Good browsing got higher and higher, and the animal's neck was stretched up and up to keep pace with the emergency. But while elongating

the neck, Nature ruined the giraffe's voice; he is now practically voiceless.[3] In order to survive, any gregarious animal
must have some means of communicating at a distance with
other members of his herd. What do you suppose the Great
Refashioner did about that? She simply increased the flexibility, and therefore the expressiveness or signaling power, of
the giraffe's tail. Nearly dumb, these herding animals now com-
municate with each other by a system of wigwagging their
tails—as doth the busy little bee, but that's too long and
involved a tail-story to tell here.

Tails, whatever other functions they may have, are generally balancers. In the bird world, of course, that is their main
function. And as the earth-bound mammal becomes aerial,
even in a limited way, the tail, so to speak, comes into its own.
(We except the bat, the only mammal capable of true flight.
Here Nature splits the tail of the family of so-called Flying
Foxes down the middle and apportions it half and half
between the two wings, leaving no tail at all.) Fortunately,
we have in Texas a tail that is the premier balancer of the
whole animal world. It is beautiful, photogenic, a thing of
beauty that is a joy forever: long, lithe, brightly ringed,
exquisite in movement, and expressive even in repose. Caco-
mistle, California mink, miner's cat, basariscus, civet, or civet
cat—all are aliases. To us he is a ringtail, and any name that
leaves the tail out is a misnomer. He's no cat, either. My own
contacts with him in the wild have been few and far apart—
only a headlighted look now and then in rocky or wooded
areas, or, around camp, a few flashlight glimpses of him skulk-
ing in the deeper shadows. Yet he returns to memory always
tail first. The tail presents the personality; for this animal's
mental processes as well as an adequate account of his emotional life could, I believe, be derived by patiently decoding and
interpreting the pantomimic eloquence of the tail.

The creature is always scaling precipitous places, venturing
out where the footing is insecure in search of small rodents

and insects. He is always negotiating narrow passages. Among trees he is an indefatigable climber, unafraid of attempting the longest, leanest limb in pursuit of his prey. He uses his tail exactly as the tightrope walker uses his balancing pole, even more expertly. He needs no net under him for he is not going to fall.

So much—or too much—of functional tails. The list is only suggestive. Nature's bizarre uses of this member condition the all-too-gullible human mind for accepting almost anything folk may tell or retell about animals' tails. Maybe that's why there's so much folklore about them.

The story which we all heard in childhood of how the fox uses his tail to rid himself of fleas was a favorite with the folk among whom I was reared, not in the forks of anybody's creek, but on the high, broad blackland prairie where Whoolia and Deer Creeks head up in the northwest corner of Falls County, Texas. According to this story, the wily creature gets tired of scratching fleas and decides to get rid of them all at once. He knows that the flea flees from water; so, in the still twilight, he sneaks down to a deep blue hole in the creek, sticks his head under the water very gradually, and the fleas, not wanting to get their feet wet, retreat to higher ground. But he then immerses his shoulders and finally his whole body, leaving no island of refuge. The fleas congregate in dismay around the root of his tail. Relentless, he hoists that bushy member and sinks it slowly down into the water, until the fleas are all huddled frantically on its very tip end. Then with a sudden, violent swish, he scatters them far and wide over the surface of the pool and swims away triumphantly, leaving them to drown. And they do drown.

There have been in circulation for centuries (and still are) two different stories tied to the rat's tail. In one of them the rat resolves himself into a sled to be dragged tailwise by another rat; while in the other story a single rat carries his nesting material faggot-wise on his back with tail drawn over the load and the tip of it clenched in his teeth to steady the burden, an obvious physical impossibility.

Most of the sled stories, however, picture the rat (occasionally, in this country, an opossum) lying flat on his back and clasping some object (usually a stolen egg) to his belly with forefeet, while his confederate in the larceny tows him along by the tail. However, this alignment of tower and towed rubs the hair the wrong way. Folk avoidance of such cruelty lies in another version in which the "sled" takes the tip of the tower's tail in *his* mouth so as to be drawn *with* instead of *against* the natural lay of the hair. This version saves hair and hide; and it economizes on ratpower, making easier pulling.

The climactic animal-sled story comes, curiously enough, from a "credible witness" who "saw it with his own eyes." In 1932 Dr. W. E. Aughinbaugh reports substantially as follows: The horse-rat was towing the sled-rat through a moon-lit patio in Caracas, Venezuela, when they came to a road-block. The "horse" mounts the obstruction, then lowers his tail to the "sled," who is pulled up and carefully let down on the other side. Aughinbaugh declares that when he told his native servants of the occurrence, they showed no surprise, saying it was *costumbre del país*, the custom of the country.[4]

Comes now the tail-end of this tail-piece. In Brazil the Indians believe that the jaguar uses his tail to lure fish within striking distance of his paw. Professor E. W. Gudger tries to pin this story down as truth or definitely dismiss it as folklore.

The great cat, ranging from our own Rio Grande to Paraguay, is represented as lying on a half-submerged log motionless except for his tail, the end of which he plops down into the water every little while. This, it is said, attracts his favorite fish to within striking distance, whereupon he knocks one out of the water with a lightning blow of his paw. "A likely story," your wet-blanketer sneers; "the plop of the tail, instead of attracting, would scare the fish away. Don't fishermen always insist upon quiet?"

But the Indian has a ready reply. "You see, Señor," he says, "the tampaquy feeds on fruits that grow along the banks of certain Brazilian streams. The ripe fruit falls with a plop into the water and there is immediately a scramble to see which one can get there first. Now the smart jaguar has noticed the feeding habits of these fish and imitates with his tail the plop of the falling fruit. The silly fish rush to the sound only to get knocked out on the bank and gobbled up."

Scientific travelers in South America have for a hundred years told this story, but not a single one of them, according to Gudger, cites an eyewitness who can be trusted. It is always "the Indians say." One scientist reports it on the word of "reputable white settlers"—no names. Another got it from an Indian guide—"a reliable informant."

Science now resorts to analogy: R. C. Murphy notes the skimmer (one of the commonest birds along the Texas coast) dipping his bill into the smooth surface of the water and back-tracking quickly to catch fish attracted by the disturbance. He notes a Brazilian kingfisher using his own defecations as lure. Catfish, he says, rise to the surface to feed upon droppings of boobies.[5] And Gudger adds to the list of analogous authenticated cases one from E. G. Heavener, Newton, North Carolina, who records a tomcat using his tail in the same way exactly that the jaguar is said to use his.[6]

Now you may pay your money and take your choice. Gudger goes on to quote approvingly a remark by W. E. Brooks, himself a distinguished scientist: "It is not safe to say that an animal does not exist, or that a known animal does not do certain things (not physically impossible) because no scientific man has as yet seen and described them."[7] This is, perhaps, a way of saying that a person without scientific training is not *necessarily* a liar.

1. *Folk Travelers*, ed. Boatright, Hudson, and Maxwell (Austin and Dallas, 1953; Texas Folklore Publication XXV), pp. 18-39.

2. Frederick Drimmer, *The Animal Kingdom* (New York, 1954), I, 92.

3. *Nature Encyclopedia*, ed. G. Clyde Fisher (New York, 1940), p. 312.

4. E. W. Gudger, "How Rats Transport Eggs: The Rat Wagon Story Traced Back to 1291 A.D.," *Scientific Monthly*, XL (1935), 415-24.

5. Robert Cushman Murphy, *Oceanic Birds of South America* (New York, 1936), II, 1177.

6. E. W. Gudger, "Does the Jaguar Use His Tail as a Lure in Fishing?" *Journal of Mammalogy*, XXVII (February, 1946), 37-49.

7. *Ibid.*

Br'er Rabbit Watches Out for Himself in Mexico

J. FRANK DOBIE

WHILE I WAS IN MEXICO CITY in 1951 writing an article on it for *Holiday* magazine, I pumped all sorts of people for views on evolving Mexican life. Thomas B. Miller received me in historic Casa Alvarado, which he and his wife maintain according to tradition, in Coyoacán, a suburb of the city. Then we had a long, leisurely talk at his downtown office. He has prospered in Mexico for many years and when he speaks of Mexico says "we," though he maintains his American perspective.

He told me of a Mexican businessman who came to him for advice on sending his son to college in the United States.

"Your son could get thorough instruction right here in Mexico City," Mr. Miller said, somewhat diplomatically.

"I'm considering something beyond knowledge," the Mexican businessman replied. "Listen! When I was a boy, every morning before I started to school here in Mexico City, my father would say, '*No te dejes*.' [Don't let anybody get ahead of you; watch out for yourself.] Then I went to a college in the States. On the very first day a professor began his class by saying: 'You are here to acquire knowledge, but you must never forget the principle of fair play. That means a regard for all fellow human beings. Success is something more than just getting ahead of everybody else.' I want my son to go where the idea of fair play is in the air."

To illustrate the old Mexican *No te dejes* idea, Mr. Miller

then told this Br'er Rabbit story. I don't know if it is in *Uncle
Remus* or not. The tales people tell reveal the tellers; Uncle
Remus and his people are not exemplars of the *No te dejes*
motive.

One day Brother Rabbit called on Brother Cockroach, a
neighbor. "My friend," he said, "you are little, but I have come
to think a great deal of you. I have ten bushels of corn to sell.
It is worth a dollar and a half a bushel on the market, but being
as it's you, you can have it for a dollar a bushel."

"Oh, thank you very much, Brother Rabbit," the Cockroach
replied. "I'd like to have a winter supply of corn."

"All right," Brother Rabbit said, "bring your wagon and
team and the ten dollars to my house along about eight o'clock
in the morning and I'll help you load the corn."

Brother Rabbit left and went over to Sister Hen's house.

"Sister Hen," he said, "you are one of the most delightful
persons on earth. The longer we are neighbors, the more I
appreciate you. I know how you like corn. I have ten bushels
to sell. It's worth a dollar and a half a bushel on the market,
but because I think so much of you, I'll let you have it for a
dollar a bushel."

"I certainly want it, Brother Rabbit," Sister Hen said. "I
thank you with all my heart for the offer."

"All right, Sister Hen, along about nine o'clock in the morning, drive your wagon and team to my house and bring the ten
dollars and we'll load up your corn."

Then Brother Rabbit went on to Mister Fox's house. He was
careful here not to get too close.

"Good morning, Mister Fox," he called out.

"Why, good morning, Brother Rabbit," Mister Fox answered. "I'll declare I'm glad to see you."

"Yes, I know you're glad to see me," Brother Rabbit said.
"You might eat me up if you could, but we've been neighbors a
long time and you never have bothered me. That's why I want

to do you a favor. I have ten bushels of corn I don't need. It's worth a dollar and a half a bushel on the market, but if you want it, I'll let you have it for a dollar a bushel."

"You know, Brother Rabbit," Mister Fox said, smiling a broad smile, "I was going to buy some corn. Your generosity makes me your servant forever."

"All right," Brother Rabbit said, "put ten dollars in your pocket and about ten o'clock tomorrow morning drive your wagon and team to my house and we'll load the corn in."

Brother Rabbit said goodbye and went on to Mr. Man's house.

"Good morning, Mr. Man," he said.

"Good morning, Brother Rabbit. I been wanting to tell you how much I appreciate your never getting into my garden."

"Yes, Mr. Man," Brother Rabbit said, "we've been good neighbors a long while. You have respected me just as I have respected you. To show how much I think of you, I've made a special trip over here to tell you that if you want ten bushels of corn you can have it at a dollar a bushel. It's selling at a dollar and a half a bushel, you know."

"Yes, I know, and I thank you, Brother Rabbit. I'll take the corn."

"All right, Mr. Man, bring your wagon and team and money to my house about eleven o'clock tomorrow morning and you shall have the corn."

The next morning bright and early, here came Brother Cockroach in his wagon, driving a good team of mules.

"Drive right into the patio and get down," Brother Rabbit called in his heartiest voice. When the mules were tied, he said, "Let's sit down and sip a little sugared coffee and visit a bit. There's no hurry. I guess you brought your money."

"Yes, here's the ten dollars," Brother Cockroach said, handing the bills over and taking a chair.

After they had sat and sipped and gossiped a while, Brother Rabbit happened to look out the window. "I'll declare," he said in a low voice, "of all people, yonder comes that old Hen. I know how you are scared of her. She won't stay long though. You just get into this oven and I'll shut the door and everything will be safe."

The Cockroach got into the earthen oven, Brother Rabbit shut the door, and Sister Hen drove up.

"Drive right into the patio here," Brother Rabbit called out. "Get down. I got something to show you. You might like a little appetizer before we eat a tortilla."

After Sister Hen hitched her team, Brother Rabbit motioned her to the oven. "When I open the door, take a peep," he said.

Sister Hen craned her neck and away over in the corner she spied the Cockroach flattened out. She made one grab. Then, holding him in her beak, she gave a knock or two against the floor and swallowed him right down. "Very nice," she said.

"I guess you brought your ten dollars."

"Here's the money," she said.

"Well, there's no hurry about loading the corn," Brother Rabbit said. "Let's have a tortilla and a little something else."

While they were having a tortilla and a little something else, Brother Rabbit happened to look out the window. "Gracious me!" he called out in alarm. "Yonder comes your worst enemy. Here, quick, before that Fox person sees you! Get in that oven. I'll shut the door and he can't even smell you."

Sister Hen dodged into the oven, Brother Rabbit shut the door, and Mister Fox drove up.

"Put your wagon and team in the patio here," Brother Fox called out. "Get down and hitch your horses and let's have a little tequila to make us feel more like loading the corn. I guess you brought your ten dollars."

"In silver," Mister Fox said, rattling the coins as he transferred them to Brother Rabbit.

While they were trying out the tequila, Brother Rabbit kept a respectable distance away from his visitor. When he saw Mister Fox wiping his mustache, he said, "By good luck, there's a little extra to go with the corn. Come over here by the oven and when I open the door look and see what you see."

He opened the door. Mister Fox took one look and one grab. He ate everything of Sister Hen but the feathers; and he was sniffing them around and tossing them up to watch them float in the air, when Brother Rabbit happened to look out the window.

"Goodness alive!" he called in a low voice. "Mr. Man is driving right up here. He has a gun, too. I see it by his side. If you go out the door, he'll shoot you. The only thing for you to do is to hide, and the safest place is that oven. I'll shut the door carefully and your enemy will never know you are around."

The Fox jumped into the oven and the door was closed when Mr. Man drove up.

"Well, you're on time," Brother Rabbit said. "I guess you want to get loaded right away. As soon as you pay me, I'll show you where to get the corn."

Mr. Man handed over the ten dollars.

"Wait a minute," Brother Rabbit said. "I know how that Fox person is always raiding your barnyard and how you are always looking for him and can't get a shot at him. Well, get your gun and have it ready."

As soon as Mr. Man got his gun, Brother Rabbit opened the oven door. There Mister Fox was squatted in the corner, trying to sink into the floor. One shot and he was dead.

Mr. Man loaded his ten bushels of corn and drove away. Brother Rabbit had forty dollars and three wagons and teams besides. He had not let anybody get ahead of him.

Recollections of an Itinerant Folklorist

STITH THOMPSON

Address to the Texas Folklore Society, May 20, 1956

MY FRIENDS, I suppose you can realize that this is a moment of great gratification for me, coming back after forty years, to see the Society that I knew in 1916 in such a flourishing condition. Most state folklore societies that I've known have started off with a great enthusiasm and then have gradually dwindled and sometimes have died. The Texas Folklore Society doesn't seem to do that at all. This means that there have been enthusiastic folklorists here all these years to keep things going. If I send my grandchildren down this way another forty or fifty years from now, I am confident that they will see a flourishing Society.

It has been a long time now since I first came to Texas. When I arrived in Austin one September morning, in 1914, I had the good luck to find a room in a nice new house, and it was only the next day that I discovered that I was living in the home of John A. Lomax. Of course, I had heard of John Lomax at Harvard, for he had already become a legend there, and I was very happy about this association. The next spring, he invited me to go with him up to Baylor for a meeting of the Texas Folklore Society. We had a pleasant time there with Dorothy Scarborough and A. J. Armstrong and the other people around Baylor. They were looking for a young, eager person as Secretary and Treasurer, and who was so young and eager as I?

On the way back on the train, Mr. Lomax said: "We have always kept the papers that are read at the Society. Wouldn't it be a good idea to get them together and publish them?" That was the way the Society's first publication was dreamed up. Frank Dobie has been quite right in saying that I hounded people for memberships until we finally raised about $150 and were able to issue this publication.

One incident about that might interest you. At the first meeting of the Society after I became Secretary, Professor Barrett Wendell was down from Harvard to speak at the Shakespeare tercentenary celebration. The University of Texas had arranged to use one of his lectures for the meeting of the Folklore Society. He seemed to be much interested in the program, and after the meeting was over, came to me and said, "This Society interests me very much. I want to contribute to it the fee which I received for this lecture." With this hundred dollars from Professor Wendell, when I left I was able to turn over a hundred-dollar Liberty Bond plus a few more dollars to Professor Robert Adger Law. This fund he finally transferred to Frank Dobie, and the results have made folklore history.

I have been asked to give here tonight some recollections of an itinerant folklorist. In my Texas days I was not yet a confirmed itinerant. To be sure, I had begun my folklore work at the University of Wisconsin, and had pursued it to some extent in Portland, Oregon, and then picked it up at the University of California, and later at Harvard, but I was still only a student, wandering from one university to another. But since those days I have had a really wandering life, pursuing wherever it would lead me this subject of folklore. If I really took you with me on all these journeys, you would certainly go to sleep or desert me—and I wouldn't want that to happen.

Two subjects I should like to bring to your attention, and I hope, as good old friends, you will forgive me for discussing them, because they are the kind of things that do not normally come before a state folklore society.

The first of these is a consideration of the various possible approaches to the study of folklore. The folklorist can do a

number of things and all of them may be good. We heard one
excellent approach illustrated today by Professor William A.
Owens, the use of folklore for fiction (as in his novel *Walking
on Borrowed Land*), and that is one of the important uses folklore can have.

Or the folklorist may be primarily a collector, going out and
picking up traditional material wherever he can find it. It is
likely that the members of a state folklore society will be
mainly of this kind if they are really active. As collectors, they
will be especially interested in the people from whom they
receive their material. They will become specialists, not in the
subjects, but in the people with whom they are working. They
will have a tendency, a very natural and commendable tendency, to think about their people as extraordinary. "These,"
they believe, "are the best people and they tell the best stories.
Nobody can sing that particular song the way my singer can
sing it." This is the approach to folklore from the point of view
of the singer, or the tale-teller, with the interest centered in
the informant.

Now the folklorist may not be a collector at all, but he may
arrange the material after it is collected so it can be made available to the public. Such arrangers may be those who issue collections and order the material so that you can easily find it in
books or periodicals. Or they may make indexes and classifica-
tions, and on the basis of these indexes, they may develop
archives, so that when people write and ask whether they have
a certain story or a certain song, they can answer intelligently.
To this task I have devoted a good part of my own life.

Some people find their chief interest in the presentation of
folklore. Thus we have singers of folksongs and tellers of folktales—all the way from the professional storyteller, who tries
to tell the tales exactly as he heard them, down to the teller of
bedtime stories or the entertainer of children in the children's
room at the library. This presentation of folklore is not my business at all. And I am thankful for this, because the presenting

of folklore gets you into all kinds of trouble. You cannot satisfy anybody. If you present it correctly, the public dislikes it, and if you change it so that the public will like it, then the folklorist is going to be dissatisfied.

Finally, there are many theories of folklore that one may be interested in. The paper we had today from Professor R. C. Stephenson, on dialogue in folklore and song, is a good example of a theoretical approach to folklore. And much more of such study needs to be done.

These, then, are some of the kinds of activity open to the folklorist when he begins his career. He cannot be all things, but must choose his road. I am quite unblushing in admitting that I have never collected any folklore myself. I have been out with collectors, for I like to go along and see them gather material. But I recognize that collecting has its own techniques and I know that I would bungle things very badly. A man like Vance Randolph is a great collector, but he was honest enough to say when he received my *Motif-Index* that he would never try to annotate his stories. "I should have made an unholy mess of it," he wrote, "if I had tried that." The folklorist then is driven to a certain amount of specialization.

Now I should like to take a few minutes to tell you, as simply as I may, about the technical job on which I have been working throughout these years, and about how I came to work on it.

Back in my Harvard graduate school days, I became interested in the general problem of what happens to a piece of European folklore—whether a tale or a song—when it is picked up by the American Indians. For instance, if the American Indian took over a French folktale, I wanted to see what happened to it. For the study of this problem two preliminary tasks were necessary. First, I had to know American Indian tales—as nearly as possible all of them. Hence I read all that were then in print, although it took me a year to do this. Second, I must know a European tale when I saw it, for you cannot write about European tales among North American Indians unless you can recognize them on sight.

Accordingly I began in a very small way at first to make notes on European tales. Gradually, however, shoeboxes full of notes began to accumulate, and by the time I was ready to do the thesis, these had grown to five or six big boxes of slips, all with various motifs I had encountered in European tales, especially those that had been commented on by scholars.

That was the status of my scholarly apparatus when I arrived in Austin. The four years in Austin were busy years, for I was doing my apprenticeship. I was learning to teach freshman composition, mark themes, and confer with students. Also I did a little work with the Texas Folklore Society, and I issued three textbooks during those four years, and tried to add a little to the $1,400 salary. At any rate, during those years I could not accomplish much folklore study. I sent off the Harvard dissertation to several publishers and wondered why they refused to publish it. I know now why they were not interested, for it was padded: the 400 pages should have been reduced to about 100.

In 1918, just at the end of the war, Mrs. Thompson and I, newly married, went to what looked to us then like greener pastures, around Colorado Springs. We had an enforced vacation because of the influenza epidemic, and accordingly I had about four months with nothing at all to do. This was a good opportunity to get out my old notes and dust them off. Then I completely rewrote that thesis on *European Tales Among the North American Indians* and boiled it down to about 150 pages, to its immense improvement. When this was published by Colorado College I sent it around to the American Indian specialists, wondering what these men would say about it. The response was most encouraging. And—considering that I was still pretty young then—I was especially gratified to receive a letter a couple of months later from *Who's Who in America;* and I have been included in their volumes ever since. This letter was my first real encouragement to go ahead in the field of folklore study.

Three years later, after an interval at the University of Maine, I was brought to Indiana University to manage freshman composition. That, as anybody who has tried it can tell you, is a man-sized job, and it was a couple of years before I could think about doing anything besides trying to keep everybody happy with teaching freshman composition in that large department. But eventually I got around to working with my notes again.

You will observe that I had already handled the American Indian tales that had been borrowed from the Europeans—but I had done nothing with the real American Indian tales, those quite uninfluenced by the European. As I began to work on this latter problem I found that I was at a loss as to the proper order in which these tale-motifs should be handled. Accordingly I went on a quest to see if anyone had ever arranged narrative motifs in a sensible order—and I soon realized that nobody had. Thus I was forced to a decision: to take six months off and arrange those motifs that I then had into some good logical order so as to know how to handle them.

It must have been the summer of 1923 when I decided to take the six months off to arrange these motifs. I made some progress, and the following summer, when I was at Northwestern University, my friend Archer Taylor came along and saw what I was doing. He encouraged me so that I came to feel this was a first-rate and important work. But he felt that I must not confine the index to just what I already had. I consulted that summer with him and his friends at the University of Chicago and each of them suggested more and more items that should be included. Before the end of the summer I had plans laid out for ten years of work. But it was agreed that I should go ahead and do this study as I had begun it with the material already in hand, so that I would have some definite nucleus for later expansion. I did this, and the next year Taylor took my manuscript of approximately 400 pages with him to Finland.

To get any point from my story at all, it is necessary to realize why it is important for folklorists to go to Finland. Ever since the Finns first became interested in their own great epic, the *Kalevala,* around 1835, that land has been a kind of center of the world for folklore studies. They have certainly carried these on with more consistent seriousness than scholars anywhere else in the world. The great man of Finnish folklore studies in that generation was Kaarle Krohn. Many of my European folklore friends took a kind of pilgrimage to Helsinki for a session with Krohn.

Thus it was that Taylor took my manuscript with him to Krohn. Soon I had a letter saying that Krohn was much pleased with it. He wanted me, however, to interrupt the work on this index long enough to undertake the revision of Aarne's classification of folktales, which was being used all over Europe as a basis for the indexing and arranging of tales. This index had been done by one of Krohn's students, Antti Aarne, in 1910, and by this time had come to be used in the various folktale archives and for the surveys of folktales being made in a number of countries. About fifteen such surveys had been made on the basis of this index and many additions were found desirable. Aarne had been planning to revise it, and then just as he was ready he suddenly died. It was this index that Krohn invited me to undertake to revise.

I am certain you can appreciate the fact that this commission was the greatest thing that could have happened to me at the time. Though I recognized the possible pitfalls such a work might present, it came to me as a challenge and I accepted. We took a year off and went to Europe, mainly to Paris and Copenhagen, and revised that index.

It should be clear that this Aarne index referred to complete folktales as items, and not to the individual motifs that go to make up the tales. Thus Cinderella and Snow White are taletypes. Now in due time I returned to my own classification of the small motifs, which I was calling a *Motif-Index of Folk-Literature*, and spent about four years reading what I had laid out to be included. Eventually, we published this *Motif-Index* in six volumes between 1932 and 1936. Then, since there were many other things to do, I left folklore for a while and issued other kinds of books. But people began to write in to me, since they knew that I was woking on the folktale, and wanted me to tell them in a letter all that was to be said about the folktale. These impossible requests drove me finally to writing the book called *The Folktale*. This treatise I worked on during the years of World War II, in the time left over from teaching the soldiers.

With the war over and *The Folktale* finished, I began to move toward a revision of the *Motif-Index*. But there had been several things keyed in to this index that had to be completed before I could get around to the revision. That is a long story which I will spare you, but I finally completed this revision last December. It represents about eight or ten fairly solid years of labor. I hope it is a good work, but I am too close to it to judge.

I should like to speak now of another aspect of this whole folktale quest besides the actual work that gets done. Along with the doing of this work, there has come the acquaintance with most of the important folklore scholars of the world. It has taken me to various places, and I hope you will be willing to share with me some of the experiences.

When we went to Europe in 1926, it was primarily to revise this index for Professor Krohn. At that time I think it will be agreed that the two outstanding folklorists in the world were Kaarle Krohn, from Finland, and Johannes Bolte, from Berlin. Bolte was the author of the five volumes of notes on Grimm's folktales—a life work. If as a young scholar I wanted to see the two great folklorists in the world, they were certainly Krohn and Bolte. In London a letter from Krohn told me that quite unexpectedly he was going to be in Copenhagen the next week and that it would be pleasant if I could come over. So we changed all our plans and I met him in Copenhagen.

After we had talked all afternoon about the plans for revision of the index, he said, "Tomorrow morning at ten o'clock let us meet at the Royal Library, in the Danish Folklore Archives." So I went down at ten o'clock—eager for new experiences, but not knowing anything about what was going to happen. There I found Krohn and the archivist of the Danish Folklore Archives and later in the day accepted the archivist's invitation for dinner with Krohn. As we were leaving the archives, Krohn remarked, "Let's not forget Bolte." So we went down, and there in the library below was the great Johannes Bolte. Then Krohn and Bolte and I, along with the archivist, went across town to a railway station and then out to the country to a pleasant little house on a lake.

And here the young American folklorist ate and talked with the two most important of his colleagues in the world. It was a wonderful experience for me. After dinner we went out to see the old church at Holte and then Krohn said, "Let us go out into the churchyard." There we visited the grave of Axel Olrik. Now Olrik, who had died about ten years before, would certainly be a third of this triumvirate of distinguished world folklorists. Standing by the side of his grave, Krohn and Bolte reminisced about Olrik, about his fine character, about what a good time they had with him, and they told anecdotes about him, and I had a feeling that somehow I was in the company of the great. And the next day I was to have another evening with these gentlemen.

A year later, from Copenhagen, I went over to Helsinki to take the manuscript of the finished work of the *Types of the Folk-Tale* to Krohn. He came in from the country to the empty house in town, and we worked there together for a week. It was the middle of summer, which means that there was practically no night at all, and we usually got together late in the morning and worked and visited until late at night. We did that for five or six days, and I had the opportunity for any number of good talks with him. As time went on, we talked very seriously about the future of folktale scholarship. One day he said to me, "I want you to carry on folktale scholarship in the next generation." I didn't take this personally, but the next day, the last day we were together, he told me, "When I was a young scholar back in 1883, I went down—much as you have done for me—to the Ducal library at Weimar, and had a week with Reinhold Köhler." He said, "You, of course, know Köhler," and of course I did, because he had been the greatest of the annotators of folktales in the 1860's and seventies and early eighties. Krohn said that the last day he was with Köhler, the old man had called him in and talked to him, and as he left, said to him, "Dr. Krohn, I am now an old man. I have spent my life working on folktales, but now can't expect to do much more. For the next generation, I am looking to you." Then Krohn turned to me, "You remember what I said to you yesterday." So, putting these two things together, I felt as if I had been entrusted with a mission. These words have stayed with me and—in hours of weariness, sometimes—have urged me on.

First and last, Mrs. Thompson and I have become acquainted with most of the folklorists in Europe. I do not know personally any of the Russian specialists, though years ago I used to have correspondence with them. But in the rest of Europe I know nearly all of them. And we spent the year 1947 going all over South America, staying in most of the capitals from three to six weeks, and became acquainted with most of the folklorists in those countries. One of the things that these men in South America were interested in was hearing just the kind of things that I have been talking to you about. They were quite isolated from the European folklorists, and when I would say something casually about a man like Krohn or Wesselski, they would want to know what kind of man he was, and were eager for anecdotes about him. They wanted some news of the folklore world. We kept a very close diary, and prepared it in such form that we could let our friends read it. Many of the European folklorists have read our South American diary, and this has brought about a good deal of correspondence between the European and South American folklorists. Thus in some way we have acted as a kind of liaison.

And I was interested, a year and a half ago when I went down to São Paulo in Brazil to an international folklore meeting, to find many Europeans now for the first time meeting the South American folklorists. Of course it was not I that brought about this meeting, but I am glad of any part we have had in interesting the Europeans in South Americans and South Americans in the Europeans. They needed each other very much.

I will end this talk by saying a little about the international organization of folklore, in which I have had to take some part. We have state folklore societies in the United States and national folklore societies in nearly every country in Europe and in South America, but there is no international folklore society. On the other hand, shortly after the war, after UNESCO was started, a division of UNESCO, the Commission for Philosophy and Humanistic Sciences, created a subdivision devoted to folklore, an International Commission for Folklore and Folk Arts, with its headquarters at that time in Paris. This International Commission has gone on, and I have taken some part in it, and at the moment I am the Vice-President. The President, Dr. Christiansen of Norway, will be at Indiana University as visiting professor next year. We had an executive meeting last September in Holland, and this gave us a good excuse for a little trip to Iceland, Copenhagen, and Holland. What this International Commission will accomplish only the future can tell.

That is pretty nearly my story. At least for the moment it has a neat ending, and for me a very moving one—the return after forty years to the university of my first teaching and to the Folklore Society to which I gave my earliest loyalty.

Dialogue in Folktale and Song

R. C. STEPHENSON

STYLE IN THE EUROPEAN FOLKTALE, being an element of structure, not of diction, must be broken down, if we study it at all,
into elements as discrete as the motifs. One of the areas in
which they may be separately considered is dialogue, which
folk artists themselves recognize as a special and all-important
problem. Zykov, a Russian folktale-teller who probably didn't
known the word "dialogue," called it "the talk." "The talk," he
said, "is the main thing [in a tale] and it's the hardest part to do.
Get one word of it wrong, and the whole thing is spoiled. It has
to move fast."[1] Now there's no certainty as to just what he
meant by "moving fast." Most likely he meant two things:
execution, or a brisk interchange that imitates the give and take
of conversation; and content, or speech unencumbered by mere
poetic or rhetorical ornament. Average shapes in folktales war-
rant this assumption, but after all it's only a guess. What we
can, though, consider with some profit is his useful term,
"the talk."

Properly speaking, the oral tale throughout is nothing but
talk, and successful talk only when made over into the idiom
and rhythms of the speaker. We go on repeating this incontest-
able fact, but we often overlook what it implies. Edwin Muir,[2]
for example, says of the Scottish Ballads, "[They] achieved
great poetry by an unconditionality which rejects, where other
literatures use, the image. In no poetry, probably, in the world,

is there less imagery than in the ballads. This is not the sign of poetic debility but of a terrific simplicity . . . which never loosens into reflection; and reflection is one of the moods in which images are given." These are eloquent words, which apply in some degree to the folktale as well as the ballad, but they miss the central point. Precisely because ballad and folktale are forms of oral art, they do largely reject the *visual* image, but they are rich, on the other hand, in what we would expect, a variety of *auditory* images; and it is the musical nature of these that makes style an analyzable function of structure.

We must further qualify Mr. Muir's assertion that the ballads (and, I add, the folktale) avoid the visual image. It is true that such striking metaphors as the gray cock (twilight) and the red cock (sunrise) in the English ballad or the white rider (day), the red rider (sunrise), and the black rider (night) in the Russian folktale are rare. But ballad and tale are full of almost imperceptible similes that have lapsed into commonplaces of folk speech. These are the heroine, in the Spanish ballad, who flies, i.e., rides, away as swift as a hawk; the hero, in the Russian tale, who goes to the mark like an arrow from the bow; the dress, in the same folktale, which shines like fire; and countless homely comparisons such as "tall as a pine," "big as a mountain, "white as snow," and the like. What folktale and ballad reject is not the visual image as such, but the unique visual image. It could hardly be otherwise, since traditional repetition would blur any images that survived, and the common memory would lose or reject any outlandish comparison. It must be remembered that the language employed is traditional, in other words a common fund of folk speech. In it figures, like idioms, are leveled. They are leveled in texture but not turned banal. For in any case they are merely the vehicle of the speaking voice, which brings them to fresh new life.

I was reminded of this the other night when listening to a folk talker.[3] A folk talker, in my definition, is a ballad singer or a folktale-teller, or a member of a ballad-singing or folktale-

telling community, when busy with mere anecdote or community or personal memories; in other words, when using the
language of the folk upon materials not yet organized into an
art form. At such a moment this language is peculiarly open to
observation, as being uninvolved in a distracting pattern. What
I noticed in it was its plainness, the quality that Mr. Muir had
in mind. It had little of the picturesqueness of peasant speech
in romantic novels. In diction and syntax it was homely but
without the spastic eccentricity of rural speech on the stage.
In idioms, above all, it was the tried, the true, the relatively
inconspicuous and even-textured usage of a whole community.
What distinguished it, then? Three things, it seemed to me:
the flowing rhythms, the comfortable pauses, and the loving,
protracted stresses. These stresses in particular set me to thinking of the ballad and the folktale, and reminded me of devices
to which they seemed to be related. It is my purpose here to
discuss two or three of the devices, petty effects, almost purely
vocal turns, in their positive and their negative use in ballad
and folktale talk.

To begin with, since, as my argument runs, figures of speech
and special syntactical devices are adapted to the tale-teller's
own rhythms and manner of delivery, they apparently come to
be identified with his, the narrative voice, as his, the narrator's
style. They are accordingly absent almost entirely from the
dialogue. Here, Mr. Muir should have noted, is where the ballad
(cognate in this to the tale) is truly devoid of ornament.
Another explanation might be made. As the *Handwörterbuch
des Deutschen Märchens* reminds us, dialogue has to carry
salutations, riddles, directions, cumulative formulas, etc., which
we find, as we would expect, in the most economical expository
form. The dialogue, in other words, is more simply functional
than the narration. But there is plenty of unspecialized talk
as well, and this, too, is, by comparison with the narrative passages, noticeably devoid of ornament. Figures like those already
mentioned, the red cock, the black rider, etc., belong to the tale-

teller, not to his characters. "Sir Patrick Spens" (58A) with its

> "Late late yestreen I saw the new moone,
> Wi the auld moone in hir arme,"

and the Spanish *Romance de la Condesita* with its

> Carta en mi corazón tengo
> que don Flores vivo está
>
> [Letters in my bosom tell me
> My Don Flores still is living],

are almost unique in putting such striking figures into dialogue. In fact, what looks like the effort to distinguish between the narrator's speech and that of his characters leaves the latter undifferentiated among themselves. Only with such motifs as the Garrulous Wife, the Crow and the Fox, the deaf man or the simpleton does there seem to be any even rudimentary attempt at characterization through dialogue. Perhaps we can recognize a national type. When Ivan in "Ivan the Peasant's Son and Fingerling of the Seven-Verst Beard" was rude to the old man who stopped and questioned him,

He went on for a short while, but he thought, "Why did I offend the old man? Old people know many things." He returned, overtook the old man, fell at his feet, and said, "Forgive me, little grandfather. I offended you out of unhappiness. I was weeping because of my trouble. For three years I have been seeking in the fields and among the herds, and nowhere can I find me a horse."

But this is any proper-spirited Russian lad at all. In the animal tales it is the same story. We know the voices of the three bears and, indeed, bears in folktales all talk, as the Russians say, *po-medviezhi*, or in the bear language. But the big bear always talks like any other he-bear, the middle-sized bear like any other she-bear, and the little bear like any other cub. This we expect. Anything else would be Romantic and impedimental, and, as Zykov put it, it would keep the talk from moving fast.

In "The Fisherman and His Wife," the fisherman who each
time, as he returns to the flounder with his wife's insatiable
demands, shakes his head and murmurs, "It's not right," is
almost alone in having a true *mot de caractère*—unless, that is,
we count English giants with their "Fe, fi, fo, fum, I smell the
blood of an Englishman," Spanish ogres with their "¡ Fo, fo, fo!
¡A carne humana me huele aquí, si no me la das te como a ti!"
and Russian *baba-yagas* with their "Fu, fu! Russkim dukhom
pakhnet!" Or unless, again, we count the frequent coarseness
of Spanish dialogue, with its strong anal complex.

Apparent as it is, in general, that the dialogue is intentionally bare of ornament—except for formulary verses—the tale-
teller often goes out of his way to underscore the fact. He will
turn an initial bit of direct discourse into mere repetition of the
introductory phrase. My only example of this at hand comes
from a North American Indian tale, "Manabozho's Birth," but
it is a beloved convention in the European tale as well: "One
day her daughter begged to go with her. 'Mother, let me go
and help you [she said].' "[4]

Along with metaphorical ornament, something much plainer,
but at the same time more important to the style of the tale, is
characteristically absent from dialogue. This is what I noticed
in my folk talker's speech. It is an emphatic repetition of adjec-
tives and adverbs, a mannerism ideally suited to translating the
superlative degree into tone and therefore into feeling. In the
ballad, likewise, which closely follows even the folktale effects
that get lost in music, repetitions of the sort are much more
common to narrative than to dialogue, even though, in either
case, they are often needed as tags to complete a line. Hence
the phrase "Late late yestreen" in the old sailor's speech is
statistically somewhat out of place, as is "Vete por una calle
oscura, oscura, y le hallarás" in the Spanish tale of "Las tres
bolitas." In the latter case the presence of this kind of repetition
in speech may be explained as formulary, since it is set off
against the later directions, "Vete por aquella puerta clara,

clara, y allí saldrán a abrirte." But with or without special
explanation, it is a feature considerably less frequent in ballad
and folktale dialogue than in narration, and therefore a sort of
negative characteristic of dialogue.

In Russian folktales the corresponding device, equally intense
and emphatic, is parataxis. Each of these devices, we may note,
is a structural, in other words an auditory, one. And parataxis,
like emphatic repetition, belongs to the narration. Where, as
happens with repetition, it appears in dialogue, there is usually
an exceptional explanation. Thus, in "Vassilisa the Fair," when
the witch remarks, "Learn too much, get too old," we forgive
her: she is being sententious. In other languages, too, proverbs
in the dialogue are likely to be paratactic. So, the tailor in the
German tale "The Gallant Tailor" remarks, "Most haste, worst
speed." To return to the Russian, in "The Three Kingdoms:
Bronze, Silver and Gold," we explain a case of parataxis as
amphibian, lying partly in the narration and partly in the
dialogue. This is a beautiful example, rather suggested than
actually stated, and involving the repetition already discussed:
"[The eagle] carried and carried Ivan till over the mountains.
'Do you want me,' said he, 'to crush you?' And over the seas.
'Do you want me,' said he, 'to drown you?' "

If the like rhetorical effect is to be found, in general, around
dialogue but not within it, there is another of which we may
say quite the opposite. Dramatic irony or, as the Spaniards
call it, "deceiving with the truth," almost of necessity belongs
to dialogue alone. A fair example of it turns up in the ballad
"Gude Wallace" (157), when an English officer, leading a
searching party, asks whether anyone has seen Wallace:

> "The man," said Wallace, "ye're looking for,
> I seed him within these days three."

There is a much better case, a witty one, in the Russian tale
"The King of the Sea and Vassilisa the Wise." Vassilisa and
the young hero are fleeing from the castle of the King of the

Sea, who sends messengers in fierce pursuit. When about to be overtaken, Vassilisa turns herself into a ruined chapel and the hero into an old priest to watch over it:

"Ho, there, old fellow [cry the pursuers]. Have you seen a stout youth and a fair maiden pass this way?"

"Yes, countrymen, I did that [the old priest replies]. It was when I was a young man still and this chapel was being built."

Similar passages are characteristic of the flight motif in general.

Finally, there is another use of dialogue which amounts to a characteristic style. This is the device of creating a scene or making a description through the implications of rapid speech. It is most common in the dramatic ballad, where the narrative passages are merely interstitial without room for set descriptions. So, in "Thomas Rymer" (37A), the Queen of Elfland paints heaven, hell, and the fairy midlands in three magical questions:

"O see ye not yon narrow road?"
. . . . .
"And see ye not that braid braid road?"
. . . . .
"And see ye not that bonny road?"

There is the same wonderful art in the *Romance de la Doncella Guerrera*. As the warrior maiden goes galloping home, we see the whole stretch of the way fly past in her words:

Campanitas de mi iglesia,
ya os oigo repicar;
puentecito, puentecito,
del río de mi lugar,
una vez te pasé virgen,
virgen te vuelvo a pasar.
Abra las puertas, mi padre,
ábralas de par en par . . . .

[Little church bells of my village
Once again I hear you peal;
Little, little bridge across the
River of my native fields,

Once I went away a virgin,
I return a virgin still . . .
Come and let me in, O father,
Let the door swing wide and free.]

A corresponding use in the folktale appears principally in
taboos. Except for the picture of the witch's hut, description
in the tale, as for oral art in general, is consistently limited to
labels. There is a fork in the road, a river, a sea, a forest, a
garden wall, a solitary tree, a palace, and so on. These are at
most goals or foci in the linear course of the narrative. But when
a ban is laid upon the hero or the heroine, suddenly a descriptive detail comes into being. "You may open any door but this
one," says Bluebeard, and all at once his palace exfoliates into
ominous architectural detail. So it is again in "Our Lady's
Child." Description in the tale is severely functional. The
descriptive stroke is added only when it is needed. The need
arises almost inevitably with a warning, i.e., in the course of
dialogue. Then, like invisible helpers, or like a self-effacing
Chinese stage-carpenter, it may swiftly sketch in a whole scene.

The features of style that I discuss are colorless minutiae.
I set them down as general impressions only, without statistical
support. An analysis of ballad dialogue by itself would reveal
much more salient components both of dramatic tone and of
structure. There are even other aspects of dialogue, an emotional
use of repetition, for example, that ballad and folktale share.
Thus, in "Hansel and Gretel," when the father asks, "Hansel,
what are you stopping to look at?" Hansel answers, "Oh, father,
I am looking at my white cat"; and, again, the next day, when
his father asks once more, "Hansel, what are you stopping to
look about you for?" he answers, "I am looking at my dove";
and we are instantly reminded of ballads. Not only this, but it
comes home to us that the very formulas, apart from aesthetic
and structural considerations, have the purpose of serving as
props to the auditory memory. However trivial, or even because
trivial, enough small observations—if not the ones I give, then

others like them—can piece together the whole complex of manner. Provided we search them out as correlates of oral delivery, they, and they alone, will give us the molecular structure of folktale style.

1. U. M. Sokolov, *Russkii Fol'klor* (Moscow, 1938), p. 315.

2. *A Note on Scottish Ballads.*

3. Some reminiscences of John William Pendergrass, tape-recordings in the possession of his daughter, Mrs. Wolfgang Michael of Austin, Texas.

4. Stith Thompson, *Tales of the North American Indians,* p. 9.

The Twelve Truths in the Spanish Southwest

WILSON M. HUDSON

IN A LETTER written to me while I was editing *The Healer of Los Olmos and Other Mexican Lore* for the Texas Folklore Society in 1951, Miss Ruth Dodson of Alice, Texas, whose contribution gave rise to the book's title, happened to mention *Las Doce Verdades del Mundo*—The Twelve Truths of the World. She thought it strange that she had not heard about *Las Doce Verdades* until about 1942, though for many years she had known the Mexicans of South Texas intimately and had made a point of learning all she could about their customs and beliefs. When questioned, her Mexican friends answered but seemed to be holding something back. Supposing that I might have some clue, she sent me a printed leaflet entitled *Las Doce Verdades del Mundo,* which she had obtained in Corpus Christi and which carried the name of a bookstore in San Antonio below the title. Several months later she sent me another leaflet obtained in Corpus Christi, this one with the label "Printed in Mexico." In the spring of 1952 two other versions were written down and sent to me by friends in El Paso, and in 1954 I took down a version in Mexico. It is my purpose here to place these five versions on record, to relate them to the tradition of the Twelve Truths, particularly as it exists among Spanish-speaking people, and to indicate the currency and significance of *Las Doce Verdades* in the Southwest.

The latest and most extensive study of the Twelve Truths

and its analogues has been published by Aurelio M. Espinosa
in the comparative notes added to his *Cuentos Populares
Españoles* in 1947.[1] It provides the annotation for tale No. 14,
"Las Doce Palabras Retorneadas," which he had collected in
Cuenca, Spain, in 1920.[2] In preparing his study Mr. Espinosa
examined a total of 221 versions of the story, song, prayer, or
conjuration of the numbers.[3] He found 52 versions in Spanish,
19 in Portuguese, 28 in Italian, 16 in French, 31 in German, 41
in English, and enough in other modern European languages
to make a total of 202. Fifteen of the Spanish versions were
from Argentina, Chile, Puerto Rico, and New Mexico, none
from old Mexico. Medieval Latin yielded twelve versions and
Late Latin three. There were also versions in Pahlavi (middle
Persian, third to ninth centuries), Pali (a dialectal descendant
of Vedic Aryan), Kirghiz (a variety of Turkic), and Hebrew.
Whenever and wherever the story or song of the numbers has
occurred, it has expressed, through a series of questions and
answers, some kind of religious doctrine. The Pahlavi version
is Zoroastrian, the Pali Buddhistic, the Kirghiz Islamic, and so
on. The questions and answers may be more or fewer than
twelve, and they may be woven into a narrative or they may
exist independently. When present in modern versions, the
narrative usually takes this form: a man is required by the
devil, or makes a pact with him, to answer a series of questions;
the man cannot answer the devil's cryptic questions ("What
is one?"), and a saint or angel answers for him. The ancient
Pahlavi version had a comparable framework; hence Mr. Espinosa regards the preliminary or enveloping narrative as a very
old feature.

In brief, Mr. Espinosa thus traces the history of the Twelve
Truths of the World: the doctrinal story or song of the numbers
was well known in the ancient Orient; in Islamic versions it
could have entered into Europe by way of Greece and Spain;
the Jewish version was Oriental in origin, and it must have
existed for a long time prior to its first recorded appearance in

the sixteenth century; in the Middle Ages Christian missionaries and priests used versions in Latin to supplant pagan,
Oriental, or possibly Jewish versions and to instil basic Christian
doctrine; in the sixteenth and seventeenth centuries distinct
Catholic and Protestant versions developed in Europe; with
the increase of religious and doctrinal emphasis the narrative
framework of the pact with the devil tended to disappear, particularly in England and Germany, though one-fourth of the
Spanish versions retain this framework. Mr. Espinosa regards
his story from Cuenca, with its poor man who is saved from
the devil by Saint Joseph's answers, as being one of the best and
most complete in the modern tradition of Europe and America.

A version of the Twelve Truths from New Mexico has an
even fuller narrative framework; it was taken down in 1931 by
José Manuel Espinosa, a son of Aurelio M. Espinosa. A poor
man obtains a rich man (who is the devil) as godfather for his
son on condition that the son be given to the godfather in
twelve years less one day and meanwhile be taught no prayers;
the devil makes the poor man rich and calls for the child at the
appointed time; he finds the door locked against him, but he
says he will not break it down if the child can recite the Twelve
Truths; pretending to be the child, the guardian angel answers
the devil's twelve questions, whereupon the devil goes away,
leaving the poor man with his riches. This tale is No. 50 in José
Espinosa's *Spanish Folk-Tales from New Mexico* (New York,
1937); No. 51 is another version of the Twelve Truths, but it
consists of questions and answers without any preliminary story.
In both versions the questions are preceded by the formula
católico y fiel cristiano (Catholic and faithful Christian), with
the result that an examination of orthodoxy or faith seems to
be taking place. The devil makes the examination in No. 50,
and he makes it just before the boy reaches twelve, the traditional age for confirmation. Since the boy has not received any
religious instruction, his guardian angel must answer for him;
he is saved from the devil and presumably confirmed in the

faith. Of the five versions that I have brought together, only the Aguirre version from El Paso has a similar religious formula of address (*cristiano católico*) and none has an enveloping narrative.

Together with these two versions from New Mexico, the five versions now to be discussed show that the Twelve Truths of Spanish tradition is current in this part of America. Just how long it has been here is conjectural; it may have come in with the early Christian missionaries, and in any event it must have spread along with Spanish influence.

Let us take first the leaflet printed in San Antonio by El Centro Comercial at 725 West Commerce Street. It is folded twice to make four leaves with print on six of the eight pages thus formed. After the title-page three separate items appear: first, on pages 3-4, "Las Doce Verdades del Mundo"; second, on page 5, "La Oración Es Como Sigue"; and third, on pages 7-8, "Oración al Señor del Saucito." Since the third item has nothing to do with *Las Doce Verdades,* I shall say nothing of it. The first two items, though printed separately, belong together.

The San Antonio version of *Las Doce Verdades* may be translated as follows:

1. Of the twelve truths of the world, tell me one?
A. One is the Holy House of Jerusalem where Christ crucified lives and reigns forevermore. Amen.
2. Tell me two?
A. The two are the two tables of Moses on which he left engraved his divine law.
3. Tell me three?
A. The three divine persons of the most blessed Trinity: Father, Son, and Holy Ghost.
4. Tell me four?
A. The four holy Gospels.
5. Tell me five?
A. The five wounds that remained in the sacred body of our Lord Jesus Christ.
6. Tell me six?
A. The six candlesticks that burn on the altar at the celebration of high mass.[4]

7. Tell me seven?

A. The seven are the seven words that Jesus Christ spoke on the holy wood of the Cross.

8. Tell me eight?

A. The eight sorrows.

9. Tell me nine?

A. The nine months that most holy Mary carried Jesus Christ in her most pure womb.

10. Tell me ten?

A. The ten are the Ten Commandments of God's law.

11. Tell me eleven?

A. The eleven are the eleven thousand virgins that attend the throne of the most blessed Trinity.

12. Tell me twelve?

A. The twelve are the twelve apostles who accompanied Jesus Christ from his preaching until his death on the Cross of Calvary.

The second part of the leaflet, which is printed under the title "La Oración Es Como Sigue" (The Prayer Is As Follows), is an enumeration of the Twelve Truths in reverse order:

The twelve apostles, the eleven thousand virgins, the Ten Commandments, the nine months, the eight sorrows, the seven words, the six candlesticks, the five wounds, the four Gospels, the three divine persons, the two tables of Moses, and the Holy House of Jerusalem where Jesus Christ lives and reigns forevermore, AMEN.

Normally this so-called prayer would be merely the last response, all others having been made in the same manner—that is, by repeating in reverse order all the numbers previously given.

The second leaflet sent me by Miss Dodson, the one printed in Mexico, is set up in very much the same format as the one from San Antonio. The phraseology is not identical, but the items in the responses are the same. The religious or doctrinal character of *Las Doce Verdades del Mundo* is emphasized by this caption following the title: "Que Son Bases Firmes de Ntra. Santa Religion"—Which Are Firm Bases of Our Holy Religion. To "La Oración," which is ordinarily the last and fullest response, is added this supplication, "me ayuden y me protejan," imploring aid of all of the entities just enumerated.

These two printed versions do not build up cumulative responses in reverse as do the versions taken down from oral tradition. Only the so-called prayer is given in this fashion. Apparently the printers wished to save paper and ink; the purchasers no doubt knew how to recite *Las Doce Verdades* properly.

The version which I recorded in Mexico gives the responses in the full, reverse order. The reciter spoke fast and could have spoken much faster; she reduced her pace to allow for the slowness of writing. In Ixtlán del Río, Nayarit, all of the adult Catholics, so I was told, know *Las Doce Verdades* by heart. It has a formula of address, but it is simply *hermano bueno* (good brother). The items in the responses are the same as those in the two printed versions, with the exception of number eight, which is given as the eight joys of Saint Joseph.

One of the two versions from El Paso was furnished me through the kindness of Soledad Pérez and Cecilia Gil de Partearroyo, who recorded it while Miss Pérez was teaching at Texas Western College and Miss Partearroyo was a graduate student there. The reciter of *Las Doce Verdades* was María Enríquez Aguirre, who had learned it in the state of Zacatecas, Mexico, before coming to El Paso. In the Aguirre version, one is given as Jesus Christ, seven as the seven joys, and eight as the eight choirs; the other items correspond with those in the Ixtlán version and the two printed versions.

Another version from El Paso I owe to Gabriel Cordova, who very generously made a search at my request. Mrs. Juana Rodríguez of El Paso recited *Las Doce Verdades* for him and then wrote it out in full. In her family it had been taught by mother to daughter for at least three generations. The Rodríguez version begins with God as the first response and then parallels the Aguirre version. Mr. Cordova found five other persons in and around El Paso who could recite *Las Doce Verdades;* they were of both sexes and varied in age from fourteen to ninety. As he

listened Mr. Cordova did not notice any responses differing
from those of Mrs. Rodríguez. It seems that *Las Doce Verdades*
is well known in the neighborhood of El Paso and that there is
little variation from one version to another.

As among the five versions from Texas and Mexico and the
two from New Mexico, there is agreement on all items except
one, seven, and eight. The differences in the first response are
really very slight; they are such as would easily arise in material
preserved by tradition, as the following listing will show:

A. *San Antonio, printed:* Una la Casa Santa de Jerusalem, donde Cristo
crucificado vive y reina por siempre jamás. Amén.

B. *Mexico, printed:* Una es, la Sta. Casa de Jerusalem donde Jesucristo
crusificado vive y reina por siempre jamás. Amén.

C. *Mexico, Ixtlán:* La Casa Santa de Jerusalén donde vives y reinas,
amén.

D. *El Paso, Aguirre:* La una que es Jesucristo que es Dios y reinará por
siempre, amén.

E. *El Paso, Rodríguez:* La una es Dios que vive y reina para siempre,
amén.

F. *New Mexico, No. 50:* La una que es de Dios, donde bajó Jesucristo a
bendecir la casa santa de Jerusalén, donde vive y reinará por siempre
jamás, amén.

G. *New Mexico, No. 51:* La una, la una que es de Dios, onde [dialectal]
bajó Jesucristo a bendecir la casa santa de Jerusalén, donde vive y
reina para siempre, amén.

Of the 202 modern versions examined by A. M. Espinosa, 148
have God for number one, as do 15 of 52 Spanish versions. The
most frequent answer for one in Spanish is the Virgin. *La Casa
Santa de Jerusalén* is the Church of the Holy Sepulchre in
Jerusalem built by Constantine and dedicated in 336; apparently Mr. Espinosa rarely met with it in Spanish, though he
found it in 6 of 19 Portuguese versions.

The seventh response in versions A, B, and C (as designated
above) is the seven "words" that Christ spoke on the cross.
The allusion is not to *words* but to *times* that Christ spoke during the crucifixion: "Father, forgive them; for they know not
what they do" (Luke 23:34); to the thief, "Verily I say unto

thee, To day shalt thou be with me in paradise" (Luke 23:43);
to Mary and to the disciple standing by, "Woman, behold thy
son!" and "Behold thy mother!" (John 19:26-27); "My God,
my God, why hast thou forsaken me?" (Matthew 27:46); "I
thirst" (John 19:28); "It is finished" (John 19:30); "Father,
into thy hands I commend my spirit" (Luke 23:46). In versions
D, E, and F the seventh response is the seven joys, by which is
meant the seven joys of Mary: Annunciation, Visitation, Nativ-
ity, Adoration of the Magi, Finding the Child Jesus in the
Temple, Resurrection, and Assumption.[5] The seven joys of Mary
have been very actively commemorated by the Franciscans,
who have a Rosary of the seven joys and also celebrate a feast
of the seven joys on the first Sunday after the octave of the
Assumption.[6] Version G of *Las Doce Verdades* has the seven
choirs for its number seven; this is unusual but not unique,
some four or five other Spanish versions having the same answer.
Spanish tradition is rather uncertain about how many choirs or
orders of angels there are, though Pope Gregory the Great
affirmed nine as the correct number.

The eighth response in versions D, E, and F is the eight
choirs. Version G has the eight joys and version C the eight
joys of Saint Joseph; this last represents a double confusion,
since tradition has established that there are seven joys and
that they are Mary's. Yet the ascription of the seven joys to
Joseph is not unknown in the recitation of the Twelve Truths.[7]
Versions A and B both state that eight stands for the eight sorrows, the word *angustias* being used instead of the much more
common *dolores*. Here is a departure from tradition that does
not seem to occur in any other version. Prominence has been
given Mary's sorrows by the Roman Missal, which calls for a
mass celebrating the seven sorrows on Friday of Passion Week
and a feast of the seven sorrows on September 15; and the sorrows are enumerated by the Breviary in the responsories of
Matins for that date.[8]

The responses on which all seven of the versions now being

compared agree need little or no comment—the two tables of
Moses, the Trinity, the four holy Gospels, the five wounds of
Christ, the six candlesticks on the altar at high mass, the nine
months of Mary's pregnancy, the Ten Commandments, the
eleven thousand virgins, and the twelve apostles. All of the
versions happen to specify the four *evangelios* (the four Gospels, the first four books of the New Testament) instead of the
less frequently met alternate, the four *evangelistas* (the four
gospel preachers—Matthew, Mark, Luke, and John). The eleven
thousand virgins were supposed to have been martyred by
Huns at Cologne along with Saint Ursula; the story of Saint
Ursula is very old, and by the end of the ninth century the
number of virgins slaughtered with her was fixed at 11,000.
Just how this figure was arrived at is unknown, but it is now
regarded as legendary or apocryphal. The foundation of the
order of Ursulines in 1535 helped to preserve the memory of
the martyred virgins of Cologne.[9] In the official Church calendar
Saint Ursula and her companions, the number unspecified, are
commemorated on October 21.[10]

Though *Las Doce Verdades del Mundo* is composed of references to religious matters deriving from the Bible, ritual, and
tradition, there is nothing to indicate that it has been given any
kind of recognized status or has been promulgated by the
Catholic Church in recent times. The Spanish-speaking people
who know it and recite it are Catholics and they apparently
consider it to be an enumeration of religious mysteries and a
very potent prayer. By naming over the mysteries they identify
themselves as initiates and at the same time they evoke and
appeal to those mysteries for aid. Such a powerful prayer
should be used only when the need is very great; so I was
warned in Ixtlán del Río. Miss Dodson was told by a Mexican
woman in Alice that near her mother's home in San Antonio
there was a woman who prayed *Las Doce Verdades* every day;
the girl's manner implied that the woman was doing something
very unwise or improper. A man who had come to Alice from

Laredo told Miss Dodson that in a bad storm his father, who was bedridden, would call the family to his bedside and they would all recite *Las Doce Verdades* together. María Aguirre of El Paso also said that *Las Doce Verdades* was good to recite in case of a storm. It is felt on both sides of the Rio Grande that this recitation or prayer is not to be used at just any time but only on special occasions when more than human aid is needed.

Las Doce Verdades may properly be used in defense against a *bruja* or witch; it belongs to the practice of counterwitchcraft. When I made a visit to El Centro Comercial in San Antonio, I found copies of it on sale along with a dozen or more other printed *oraciones* or prayers. The clerk told me that since 1933, when he began to work in another San Antonio bookstore, he must have sold thousands of copies of *Las Doce Verdades*. People who believe themselves to be bewitched buy it. While I was talking to him, a woman came in with her left shoulder drawn up and her head turned to that side; she bought a copy and went out, perhaps to free herself from the influence of some *bruja*.

Miss Dodson wrote me a story of how *Las Doce Verdades* was used to deal with a witch. Once near Alice two Mexican families were camped out while grubbing brush. One night two boys took a walk away from camp; they kept on until they heard what sounded like two women talking. This sound led them to a big oak tree, where they expected to see people camped, but no one was in sight. The voices were coming from two *lechuzas* (screech owls) up in the tree. One flew away, but when one of the boys began to recite *Las Doce Verdades* the second *lechuza* fluttered to the ground helpless. The boys caught it, and at once it turned into a little woman about two feet high. She begged them to let her go, saying that she had a family of small children and was simply passing through the country with no intention of doing any harm. They took her back to camp and put her in a cage, but in the morning the cage was empty.

There can be little doubt that *Las Doce Verdades* was
brought into New Mexico and Texas from old Mexico. It was
part of the Spaniards' lore when they occupied and controlled
these regions. How long it has been current here no one can say.
At the present time it seems to be widely known, and recently
its spread has been aided by the printing press, which is still
turning out copies for sale. Because of its special significance
as a prayer, it is likely to remain current among Spanish-
speaking Catholics for a long time. And, it might be added,
north of the Rio Grande there exist side by side with it English[11]
and Hebrew[12] versions of essentially the same thing. Those who
say over *Las Doce Verdades* in Spanish, sing "The Twelve
Apostles" or "Green Grow the Rushes" in English, or recite
"Ehad Mi Yodea" in Hebrew at the close of the Seder on Pass-
over Eve are all giving expression to a folk tradition going back
to the ancient Orient.

1. II, 111-43. This collection was first published in three volumes,
1923-26, at Stanford, without notes. The edition with notes appeared at
Madrid, 1946-47, in three volumes. In 1930 Mr. Espinosa had published
an article based on fewer variants than the final study: "Origen Oriental
y Desarrollo Histórico del Cuento de las Doce Palabras Retorneadas,"
Revista de Filología Español, XVII, 390-413.

2. The word *retorneadas* in the title has no exact English equivalent;
it means "well-turned" or "well-fashioned"—hence "perfect."

3. Tales of the type of the Twelve Truths have been assigned classification numbers by Boggs, 2045, and Taylor, 2010. Aarne-Thompson tale
type 812, the devil's riddle, is related. Thompson assigns motif number
Z 21.2 to "Ehad Mi Yodea"; see my last footnote below. Other relevant
motif numbers in Thompson are H 602 (symbolic meaning of numbers),
H 603 (symbolic interpretation of playing cards), and Z 71 (formulistic
numbers).

4. The word *candelabros* has been translated by *candlesticks* instead
of *candelabra* to prevent misreading. A multiple candle holder may not
be placed on the altar; at high mass six candles are used, three on either
side. (See *The Catholic Encyclopedia*, I, 350c-d.) The Latin *candelabrum*
as adopted by English or modified by Spanish may indicate an ornamental
candlestick holding a single candle.

5. *The New Catholic Dictionary*, s.v. "Seven Joys of Mary."

6. See *The Catholic Encyclopedia*, XIII, 76d, where it is stated that the

Franciscan *Missale Romano-Seraphicum* contains "many proper masses not found in the Roman Missal."

7. See *Cuentos Populares Españoles*, II, 130, under the discussion of the seventh response.

8. The Breviary gives the occasions of Mary's sorrows as follows: Simeon's prophecy, flight into Egypt, loss of the Holy Child at Jerusalem, meeting Jesus on the road to Calvary, standing at the foot of the cross, the removal of Jesus from the cross, and his burial.

9. See *The Catholic Encyclopedia*, XV, 225a-28a.

10. Roman Missal, Oct. 21.

11. For some English versions of "The Twelve Apostles," or "The Ten Commandments" as it is also known, see No. 207 in Cecil J. Sharp's *English Folk Songs from the Southern Appalachians* (London, 1932). "Green Grow the Rushes" is of frequent occurrence in song books edited for young people; see, for example, *Sing It Again* (Delaware, Ohio: The National Conference of the Methodist Youth Fellowship, through the Co-operative Recreation Service, n.d.), p. 20; also, *Song Fest*, ed. Dick and Beth Best (New York: Oliver Durrell, Inc., ca. 1948), pp. 56-57. This last is said to be composed of "Songs sung by Intercollegiate Outing Club Association, founded in 1932." Today almost any group of college students can sing "Green Grow the Rushes," but for the most part they are at a loss when asked to explain the riddle-like responses. In fact, a knowledge of the earlier forms of the song is required, and even then it is hard to be sure of all the allusions. "One is one and all alone" stands for God; "the lily-white boys clothed all in green" are probably Jesus and John the Baptist; the three "rivals" might be the three Magi ("strangers" in some older versions), who rivaled one another in bringing gifts to the infant Jesus; the "gospelmakers" are Matthew, Mark, Luke, and John; what "the five symbols at your door" refers to I do not know; the six "proud walkers" may be a substitute for the six "cheerful waiters," understood as the six pitchers of water that Jesus turned into wine at the wedding in Cana of Galilee (John 2:6); the "seven stars in the sky" are probably the seven stars of Revelation 1:20, which are angels of the seven churches; the eight "April rainers" is a verbal substitution for the older "Archangels"; the "nine white shiners" are probably the nine orders of angels in their radiant robes ("the nine who dress so fine" in one of Sharp's versions); the Ten Commandments are sure, and so are the twelve apostles; the "eleven who went to Heaven" are the apostles, excluding Judas, who went to Hell. See William Wells Newell's pioneer article, "The Carol of the Twelve Numbers," *Journal of American Folk-Lore*, IV (1891), 215-20. Another semireligious song of the numbers in English is "A Deck of Cards"; records of this by Tex Ritter, T. Texas Tyler, and Phil Harris were heard on jukeboxes about four years ago. The ascription of symbolic meaning to playing cards has its history too;

see Johannes Bolte, "Eine geistliche Auslegung des Kartenspiels," *Zeitschrift des Vereins für Volkskunde*, XI (1901), 376-406, which gives a much wider treatment of the story or song of numbers than its title indicates.

12. On "Ehad Mi Yodea" see Archer Taylor, *s.v.* "Formelmärchen," in *Handwörterbuch des deutschen Märchens*, pp. 171-74. "Ehad Mi Yodea" first appeared in the Prague edition of the *Sepher Haggadah*, 1590, though it is generally supposed to be much older. It has thirteen numbers: one God, the two tables of Moses, the three patriarchs (Abraham, Isaac, and Jacob), the four mothers of Israel (Sarah, Rebekah, Leah, and Rachel), the five books of Moses (the Pentateuch), the six books of Mishnah (traditional headings for the study of Jewish laws and customs), the seven days of the week, the eight days of circumcision, the nine months of pregnancy, the Ten Commandments, the eleven stars of Joseph's dream (which bowed down to him, Gen. 37:9), the twelve tribes of Israel, and the thirteen attributes of God.

To Whom God Wishes to Give

A Tale of Old Mexico in English Ballad Stanzas

JOSEPH W. HENDREN

1

Now you shall hear a curious thing
  Which happened long ago
In and about a little town
  Of Old Mexico,

Wherein a prosperous merchant lived,
  Chipper and spry Miguel.
He owned a store, and all agreed
  He ran his business well.

Quite shrewd he was in trades and deals,
  And mostly on the level;
He got his money, people said,
  By working like the devil.

Pedro, friend of the brisk Miguel,
  Was a loafer of renown,
Well known to all the people as
  The laziest man in town.

What Pedro did with all his time
  Few but his wife could say;
He took life easy, that was sure,
  Throughout each drowsy day.

Earlier he retired to bed

Than is the wont of men,
Mumbling instructions to his wife
    To wake him up at ten.

Once in his bedroom Pedro hit
    The straw with keen delight,
Nuzzled his pillow once or twice
    And went out like a light.

He ate his breakfast propped in bed,
    So great was his inertion,
And then required a peaceful nap
    To rest from his exertion.

2

The able owner of the store,
    Cash-on-the-barrel Miguel,
Except for Pedro's unpaid bills
    Was doing fairly well.

For Pedro was in sad arrears,
    Which steadily grew sadder
Until Miguel, at first annoyed,
    Grew mad, and then still madder.

He sent his wife to Pedro's house,
    Some way across the hills
With a message, "Friend, I'm sorry, but
    You've got to pay your bills.

"And if, as you are used to say,
    You don't possess a dime,
Come help me haul my rocks—I'll give
    You credit for your time."

"Advise your husband not to fret,"
    The lazy one replied.
"I can't haul rocks, but tell the fool

To throw his cares aside.

"Some gift from God must help me soon
    To square accounts, I'm sure.
There's many a way to meet a debt
    In spite of being poor.

"To whom God means to give, He'll give,
    Bad fortunes to amend,
Even if through the window He
    Must put it in, my friend."

3

So matters rested for a time;
    Eventless days dreamed by,
Until for lack of any rain
    The poor man's spring went dry.

Now moisture is, for man or wife,
    A rather urgent matter,
And Pedro soon was forced to look
    About in quest of water.

He followed up a forest path
    Toward where, on higher ground,
He hoped some mountain spring of running
    Water could be found.

And while a tiny streamlet he
    Was tracing to its source,
He heard, approaching up the trail,
    The hoofbeats of a horse.

An aged señor Pedro saw,
    As he cast a glance behind,
Mounted upon a runaway
    And coming like the wind.

Right here the lazy man performed

A most unusual deed:
He deftly seized the bridle rein
  And stopped the frightened steed.

The rider was superbly dressed;
  He had a long white beard
And in his eyes a piercing look
  That Pedro slightly feared.

But then the stranger spoke him fair—
  With simple dignity
Thanked him for his courageous act
  In such a jeopardy.

And in his gratitude declared
  A secret he'd unfold
Of where a rich *tatema* lay
  Beneath the forest mold.

A *tatema* is a fabulous thing,
  A buried treasure store
Revealed by supernatural means
  To one man and no more.

A treasure he alone can touch—
  There can be no transmission
To others' hands without the lucky
  Man's express permission.

"Move that flat rock," the stranger said,
  "And you will find a treasure
Under the oak leaves." Pedro smiled.
  "Sir, that would be a pleasure."

His musings on the dried-up spring
  Were now completely banished.
And while he stooped to move the rock,
  The horse and rider vanished.

The digger scratched away the leaves

With frequent stops for rest,
For digging's devilish on the back
And ants a cursed pest.

But what eventually met his eyes
Would gladden any heart:
Coin!—six full chests of it—*Dios!*
Enough to fill a cart.

But Pedro had no cart, and so
Without a shrug or frown
He pocketed some silver coins
And slouched on into town.

On reaching home, for sheer fatigue
He stretched in bed, full length,
And took a long siesta to
Recuperate his strength.

4

When he rose yawning from his couch,
The sun had nearly set,
And jingling coins reminded the
Poor fellow of his debt.

"Tomorrow take this silver to
Miguel," he told his spouse.
And duly she delivered it
At his *compadre's* house.

Miguel was grateful for the cash
And just a bit surprised.
My lazy friend's been up to
Something new, the man surmised.

The money? *Diablo!* One thing's sure—
He never worked to earn it.
Well, if he's got a secret I'll

Be hanged if I don't learn it.

An easy way to gain some coin
    Is not a cause for sorrow—
I think I'd better visit my
    Compadre on the morrow.

Betimes he reached the hut, for he
    Was spry as any rabbit—
And had to wait till Pedro woke
    At ten, as was his habit.

Put to the question, Pedro neither
    Boasted nor demurred;
He simply told him everything
    Just as it had occurred.

"*Mi madre!*" gasped Miguel. "If buried
    Treasure you have found,
Why did you go away, you dunce,
    And leave it in the ground?"

His lazy friend responded with
    A slow, congenial smile,
"Begad, I couldn't carry it;
    It's nearly half a mile.

"But, *mi amigo*, you have two
    Good mules," continued he;
"If you'll help tote the boxes home,
    We'll split it evenly—

"A half for you, and half for me."
    "You mean that?" cried Miguel;
"Saint Francis! It's the soundest deal
    That ever I heard tell.

"Now, let us plan our strategy:
    We'll not need any tools;
I'll meet you here an hour before

Midnight, and bring the mules—

"You need not walk a step."—"Suits me,"
   Replied the lazy one.
"And now I think we'd better catch
   Some sleep before the fun."

They parted and good Pedro slept.
   About eleven, too,
His wife aroused him from his bed,
   As she'd been told to do.

But when no step of mule was heard
   Nor any knock on door,
The drowsy Pedro closed his eyes
   And slumbered as before.

At midnight, now in some alarm,
   His wife shook him awake,
Imploring him to search within
   The woods, for Heaven's sake

For fear his crafty friend might toss
   His friendship on the shelf,
And pack the treasure on his mules
   Entirely for himself.

"Go back to bed," the husband said,
   "There is no cause for fright,
Nor do I wish to be disturbed
   At this hour of the night.

"To whom God means to give, He'll give,
   Be virtue or be sin,
Even if through the window hole
   He has to put it in."

5

The wife had ample reason, though,

For her anxiety.
Miguel, sore tempted, had indeed
    Behaved abominably.

He guessed his friend would sleep all night
    And—well, to summarize,
He figured he would go alone
    And cash in on the prize.

I've worked hard all my life, thought he,
    That's why I have the mules
And he has none—why must such riches
    Be controlled by fools?

Besides, how can a shiftless lout
    Make proper use of money?
Pedro a glittering millionaire!
    The whole idea's funny.

And so with mules and servants and
    With motives gross and tawdry,
He went to play this scurvy trick
    Upon his old *compadre*.

To find the place was easy, from
    Pedro's precise account.
And when he saw the rock, Miguel
    Gave orders to dismount.

The servants brushed aside the leaves,
    Opened the chests—God's blood!
Instead of coins they found a mass
    Of evil-smelling mud.

The storekeeper was so surprised,
    And disappointed too,
He stood there stupefied, like one
    Who knows not what to do.

Till anger got the upper hand.

Carramba! He would go
And have revenge upon that lazy,
    Lying fraud, Pedro.

The stuff was loaded on the mules,
    A heavy, awkward chore.
That done, the little cavalcade
    Trailed straight to Pedro's door.

They emptied all the boxes then,
    And heaped the mud up high
Against the door and window, till
    The place looked like a sty.

Which nefarious operation was
    Performed without a sound,
The sleepers never dreaming such
    Despoilers were around.

6

But when Señora rose, soon after
    Daylight, she was shocked
To find the door and window of her
    Hut securely blocked.

She called her husband—he was known
    To help her in a pinch;
No use—the door could not be forced
    To budge a single inch.

So next they tried the window, where
    Results were better far.
They shoved the shutter something like
    An inch or two ajar.

Which being done, these humble folk
    Beheld a dazzling thing:
A jingling shower of silver coins
    Flowed through the opening.

With chirps of joy the eager wife
    Opened the window wider
And sidestepped as a mighty pile
    Of coin poured in beside her.

"To whom God wishes to give, He'll give,"
    Quoth Pedro to his wife.
"You're right as rain, for once," said she,
    "I'll swear upon my life."

No task at all for her it seemed
    To scramble up the mound,
Wriggle across the window sill
    And slide out to the ground.

And there against the door she saw
    Coins heaped up to the latch.
This was a poor man's dream come true.
    Kind Heaven! What a catch!

The woman set to work at once
    To move the coin inside
While Pedro beamed with some degree
    Of patriarchal pride.

And when the last *centavo* had
    Been raked into its place,
Tired Pedro slipped into his bed
    With soporific grace.

He had his breakfast there, of course,
    Before he fell asleep,
Telling his patient wife to take
    Some money from the heap.

"Off to Miguel's emporium—
    Buy what you need," said he;
"We're mighty short of food and clothes,
    We'll throw a little spree."

The woman lugged a hefty purse
   Of silver to the store
And ordered with a flourish she
   Had never shown of yore.

Not lost upon the keeper of
   The store was this display.
He was a jealous man, and yet
   Was pleased that she could pay.

He recognized the money too,
   Not without some regrets—
It was the same kind she had used
   Before to square her debts.

Afterward, when Miguel had turned
   To rearrange a shelf,
He repeated an old proverb rather
   Wryly to himself.

"To whom God means to give, He'll give,
   No matter what betide,
Even if through the window He
   Must shove the stuff inside.

"But who am I to question any
   Deed which *Dios* wills?
At last that rascal Pedro has
   The means to pay his bills."

Based on a Mexican folktale related by Wilson M. Hudson in *The Healer of Los Olmos*, Southern Methodist University Press, 1951.

Tales of the Kansas City, Mexico and Orient Railroad

VICTOR J. SMITH

THE MERRY MONTH OF MAY, 1912, was made still more jubilant in San Angelo, Texas, by the enthusiastic blowing of whistles and the ringing of bells. A long-sought goal had been reached as the Kansas City, Mexico and Orient Railroad steamed its first train into the City of the Conchos, having come all the way from Emporia, Kansas. During the following years it was both my fortune and my misfortune to live near the K.C.M.&O., travel on it, or observe it from the bucking front seat of a Model T Ford.

I heard whistles blow again to announce the arrival of the first passenger train from Fort Stockton, and yet again to celebrate the rails building into Alpine. By the time the road was completed to Presidio and connected with the Mexican Orient by bridge over the Rio Grande, I was living in Alpine and making trips to San Angelo and other points on the line in connection with Interscholastic League and other school activities.

Now that the ambitious building program was complete, J. M. Pouncey, editor of the Alpine *Industrial News,* waxed eloquent. "Time will come," he editorialized, "when solid Pullman trains will stop at Alpine en route to the West Coast of Mexico." "That may be true," remarked a local cowman, "but they will be side door Pullmans stoppin' at the loadin' pens."

Map reading classes for aviators during World War II discussed the "new" method of determining the shortest flight between two points of travel by stretching a string about a globe. Those who had dreamed of the Orient Railroad, however, had many years before used the same device to prove that the shortest route from the Kansas City freight terminals to cheap deep water shipping was the route of the K.C.M.&O. to the Pacific. Closing the gap between Chihuahua and the coast was, and still is, a dream for the future. For many years the Orient languished among dry pastures and flat-tire boom towns, through governmental operation and bankruptcy. Otherwise, it was said, the road did very well. "The trouble with the Orient," a cowboy remarked, "was it didn't start nowhere, it didn't go nowhere and there wasn't nothin' between." As a member of the Alpine Chamber of Commerce I have always resented that statement.

As might have been expected, a railroad situation which saw passenger trains discontinued, mixed trains operated, doodlebugs experimented with, doodlebugs discontinued and mixed trains reduced to three runs per week, not to mention somewhat lackadaisical operation and low morale on the part of some of the employees, would develop stories, anecdotes, and railroad gossip the nature of which is amusing, ridiculous, and sometimes fantastic. At times these items are reminiscent of Thomas W. Jackson's *On a Slow Train Through Arkansaw*, but always with the flavor of West Texas. Now almost lost, save in the memory of a few old-timers, are a group of tales centering about the slowness of the service or the small talk which made up the long hours of travel or of waiting in stations.

J. Roy Spence tells of delivering a new automobile to Fort Stockton, then taking the train for the 65-mile trip back to Alpine at 7:30 P.M. and arriving home at 3:30 A.M., having helped load cattle at Hovey to speed up the trip. He also relates how traveling men took the train out of San Angelo, calling upon their customers at every station with time to spare before the engineer "whistled up his passengers."

In spite of its isolation, Hovey is one of the most frequently mentioned stops on the line, as loadings of cattle were made there from the Kokernut and other near-by ranches. The railroad agent at Hovey had been bawled out a time or two for doing things without orders out there in the free spaces "West of the Pecos." One day the train dispatcher at San Angelo received the following telegram: BULL CHASING BRAKEMAN IN DIRECTION OF ALPINE. PLEASE WIRE INSTRUCTIONS.

Miss Anne Aynesworth, a life member of the Texas Folklore Society when life memberships were ten dollars a throw, wrote an essay recounting her vivid experiences on the mixed train to San Angelo. She tells how the oil lamps in the coach section tipped crazily, spilling coal oil on her new spring hat and finally going out, leaving the small group of passengers in the dark for miles. I was reminded again of the Arkansas train where the brakeman called, "Choose your partners for the tunnel." Miss Aynesworth's altogether proper but interesting essay is now a collector's item. Another passenger tells how the headlight on the engine went out near Hovey and how those aboard patiently awaited the hour of dawn before venturing to proceed to Fort Stockton.

Items reflecting how wonderfully accommodating the entire train crew was have been related again and again. A lady's hat blew out of the train window. The conductor obligingly stopped the train, backed up, and rescued the headgear. Once when my wife went to the depot in Alpine she forgot a carefully packed lunch. Hearing of her difficulty, the agent held the train while a friend drove a Model T Ford at a mad 18 miles per hour to secure the missing package. She thanked the trainmen, who sat around another half-hour for good measure before leaving the station. Mrs. Elton Miles, Alpine, reports the train frequently stopped along the old ranch roads to assist motorists in trouble; trainmen patched tires or corrected engine trouble in a most helpful manner. This has been a matter of much embarrassment to me, since I had passed the train many times when it was broken down without its having occurred to me to stop and assist the train crew to get rolling again.

The Pecos River bridge seemed to be a favorite unscheduled stop on the accommodation unlimited. One man tells how a party of hunters flagged the train at the bridge and how the train crew assisted them to dispose of a large campfire meal. Another traveler told me a similar story, but this time it was a fish fry for the engineer and fireman. He even suggested that these stops had something to do with overtime pay. "Besides," a brakeman said, "we want to show the government that they can't run a railroad."

I once stalled in a Model T at the ranch road crossing north of Hovey—out of gas on a cold night. Word went in to Alpine concerning my predicament and, in spite of rigid rules to the contrary, out came a five-gallon can of gasoline, postage free by local freight. Even then the car wouldn't hand crank. A ranch hand said the car acted as if it had been subjected to *el ojo* (evil eye) while all the while we had been blaming Henry Ford. We finally poured hot coffee from a thermos jug over the carburetor. Never did human being respond to the stimulating effects of hot coffee as did that Ford car.

I happened to be a passenger on the first new doodlebug to leave Alpine for points north. True to the traditions of the road, the conductor stopped the car to assist a passenger in collecting some of the interesting desert plants which grew in abundance along the right of way.

At an earlier period in Orient history I had chanced to transfer from the mixed to the first postwar passenger train out of Fort Stockton. A woman boarded the train with her ten-year-old son, saying, "Johnnie never seen a passenger train before and I wanted him to go through." Ah yes! Here was the first organized educational unit with "culminating activity."

Conductors on the doodlebug and other trains were always interesting and intelligent. I especially remember traveling with one who was a genuine booster for the West as well as an

entertainer. He lectured enthusiastically upon points of historic
and local interest en route. Near the Achabuche Hills he
pointed out Holy Mountain, which, due to the accidental distribution of vegetation, formed a huge series of letters against
the caliche background, a somewhat shaky H followed by
O L Y. After his comments to the passengers he said to me
somewhat ruefully, "I tried to get the section foreman to go up
there and plant a better cross on the H but he would have to
do it on his own time and wouldn't move a dagger." His speech
as we entered Mertzon was such a glowing account of that city
and its surroundings that it brought forth comment from a lady
passenger. "Land sakes!" she said. "I was a-goin' to get off here
but it must be Atlantic City the way he talks."

The climax of this conductor's oratory was reached, however, as the car entered San Angelo. Here he grew eloquent on
the miles of running water (this was some years ago), the
enterprise of the West, the hospitality of the city, population
trends, commercial opportunities, schools, et cetera, et cetera.
But the comment I remember best was the one related to the
churches. "San Angelo," he said, "has 23 churches, all working
to beat the devil."

At another time one of the less talkative of the conductors
in the same situation simply called, "San Angelo! Change for
Carlsbad and Ballinger!" Then, walking the length of the short
passenger compartment, he announced, "Same at this end."
As the car slowed for the San Angelo depot a male passenger,
now fully aroused after a not strangely drowsy journey, called,
"Conductor, didn't I give you a good cigar to make sure I got off
at Big Lake?" The conductor, who had been through quite a
scrimmage some miles back, answered in surprise: "My gosh!
Who *was* that we put off at Big Lake?"

O. L. Sims, of Sims Valley and Paint Rock, tells an interesting story of one Briar Dugan, foreman of a construction crew
working near Barnhart, where blasting was required for a series
of railroad cuts. Briar prided himself upon being quick and

constantly alert to the danger of his occupation. As he sat confidently on a powder keg one noon hour he carefully lit his pipe for an after-lunch smoke. Most unfortunately, however, the lighted match broke and fell into an open keg of powder. "Do you know," said the boasting Briar, "for a moment that had me worried. I wasn't too sure I could get away from that explosion in time."

Boom days accompanied the original building of the railroad, even through the deserts of West Texas. Almost invariably the depot was placed far from the center of original business activity; witness Fort Stockton, Alpine, Presidio, and other towns. It was hinted that real estate dealings had influenced these locations. The stock answer of the railroad men, however, to the question, "Why do they build the depot so far from town?" was, "They wanted to get it near the railroad." At Fort Stockton the town slowly prospered and the two almost separate villages merged into one greater community. At Presidio, however, it has been almost impossible to heal the wounds which resulted from the establishment of two rival communities. A few years ago I visited the Presidio schools. At that time there were *two* distinct and separate Parent-Teachers' Associations, fortunately careful to meet on different days, but each earnestly pursuing whatever the P.-T.A. is supposed to pursue. Each of these organizations had its full quota of officers, committees, and delegates—and the consequent filling out of reports. It is pleasing to report that the children were doing nicely and that the superintendent of schools had no gray hairs. It might be added, however, that he was as bald as an egg at the time. The agent at Presidio relates that a prospective passenger came to his window and asked for a round-trip ticket. "Where to?" asked the agent. "Back here, of course," replied the customer.

One of the kindly conductors is said to have conducted school at Hovey. He is credited with going to the schoolhouse, assigning lessons, collecting papers, and checking the progress of the children, all within the normal time of the train stop.

Steam trains frequently picked up an extra fireman at Hovey to assist the weary crew in shoveling coal into the hungry firebox en route "up the hill" to Alpine. Going the other way the engineer said, "I get her started if I can and she rolls all the way." When asked if the downgrade speed might not result in a collision he said, "Nope, can't happen. They ain't but one train."

By far the most frequent comments from travelers related to the slow train theme. The following is reminiscent of one of the Artemus Ward stories but, as usual, has the West Texas setting: A ranchman was traveling to Chancellor (one of the two-story depots which had promised a city but was later moved to McCamey after the oil strike). With an exaggerated air of politeness he asked the conductor if the railroad would accept a kindly suggestion from a passenger. He was assured somewhat guardedly that it would. "Well," said the cowman, "it seems to me that those shop boys at Angelo ought to unhitch the cowcatcher from the front, back the last car into the roundhouse and wire it to the rear end. We ain't liable," he continued, "to catch up with no cows but what's to prevent one walkin' in the back door and hookin' a passenger?"

Another yarn reports that a calf was killed on the right of way. Emphasis is placed upon the fact that the calf was a lifelong cripple; otherwise it would never have been overtaken by the train. Damages were in order. "We know," wrote the claim agent to the ranch owner, "that you have suffered some small loss in the death of this animal but we must remind you that livestock has no right to pasture on the right of way of the road. Such grazing constitutes trespass. Legally you, the owner of the calf, also become a trespasser. It is not our desire," the agent continued, "to take this case to court and give you trouble. For this reason we are requesting that you write us and indicate what you believe to be a reasonable settlement between yourself and the railroad." To the surprise of the claim agent he received a reply which said, "It's been a bad year and I can't pay you much but if you won't sue I'll pay you $7.25."

I have suggested some parallelism between the paperback *On a Slow Train Through Arkansaw* and the Orient version of similar theme. A careful comparison between the two will show several similar yarns based upon Jackson's theme of "Shall we take the train or are you in a hurry?" The Arkansas stories of slowness—catching up with those cows again and again—is echoed in Texas, as is the story of the young butcher boy who ended the run as an old man. The West Texas version, however, has a new doctor, somewhat embarrassed because of his youth and inexperience, take the train at San Angelo for his first location, Fort Davis. "All was well," the story goes; "by the time he arrived at Alpine he was a middle-aged M.D." In Arkansas the conductors had difficulty with half-fare passengers becoming adults, and hence full-fare passengers, before the end of the trip. It is said that a babe in arms was on the train leaving Emporia. At Sweetwater his mother missed him, only to find that he was in the baggage car shooting craps with the news butch—with a safety razor as stakes.

But back to Jackson's "Arkansaw" book. Since its publication in 1903 seven million copies are reported to have been sold. The Union News Company at the peak of sales was disposing of 1,000 copies per day. The Cincinnati and Ohio Railroad magazine, *Tracks,* in an article by Davis Brittle, recounts the success of Jackson's first volume entitled *Corn by the Carload,* and states that the thirteen Jackson publications together had sales of some fifteen million copies.

In a letter dated March 11, 1953, Harry G. Jackson, son of Thomas W. Jackson, informs me that his father was a railroad man for twenty-five years in Texas (M.-K.-T.) and Arkansas, having lived in Denison and later setting up in Chicago his own publishing house, which is still in business. Gone now, though, as Brittle reports, are the days of the news butch and his huge jokebook sales. The Arkansas rustic and his slow train have been shouldered (bare shouldered, that is) off the newsstands.

Change has also come over the old K.C.M.&O. The progressive Santa Fe is now the owner of the once bankrupt Orient. Railroad rules and efficiency prevail, crews are unionized, workmen have retirement and pension rights, time schedules prevail. "The Grand Canyon Line" appears on underpasses, ballast has been added, and new equipment rolls. Along the route once traveled by Mendoza and his Spanish explorers, one now sees huge diesels pulling long freights south out of San Angelo, some of the cars destined for Chihuahua and Mexico City. I commented upon this sign of progress to the section foreman at Alpine. "Wasn't so much progress," he commented, "as the fact that all the wells got low and we couldn't tank up the steam trains."

During World War I the picturesque Santa Fe depot at San Angelo was abandoned in favor of a Union Depot, the begrimed Orient brick structure. Here, as happened long ago in Arkansas, a train bulletin announced:

SANTA FE—3 hours late, account washout.

ORIENT—On time, cause unknown.

The Orient train *did* come in on time but the loafers refused to believe it. One said, "It's yeste'day's train."

Christ in the Big Bend

ELTON R. MILES

To the Texas Border Mexican, the day of miracles is not done. The world to him is not only the everyday world of chopping weeds and running river water down rows of irrigated canta- loupes, or skimming the rich foam from the *candalia* boiler. It is also a world of magic, both white magic and black magic.

Where the twin towns of Presidio, Texas, and Ojinaga, Mexico, face each other across the Big Bend in the Rio Grande is a world where the devil has laid with his own hands the stone foundation of the shambling international bridge; it is a world where no other than Christ himself walks the fields at night to bring the infrequent rain that is necessary to survival. Though the Border Mexican may not positively affirm these miracles, he will admit no absolute denial when he shrugs and remarks, "Quién sabe?"

A few miles down the river from Ojinaga, a mountain stares across the valley to the Texas desert and the distant Shafter range. This mountain is called El Cerrito de la Santa Cruz— The Little Hill of the Holy Cross—and on its peak stands a small stone chapel with a dirt roof. The chapel houses three crosses used by the valley farmers in Holy Cross Day celebra- tions. And the chapel stands just above a cave in the face of the cliff where the devil is said to have his dwelling place.

The presence of this chapel on El Cerrito de la Santa Cruz is explained in two separate legends. One of these legends says

171

that the devil used to emerge from his cave, terrorize the people, and wither the crops with his hot breath. It says that an Ojinaga priest drove the devil into his cave to stay by confronting him with a homemade cross, and that he then built a shrine above the cave in which to place the cross so that the devil would remain forever imprisoned in his grotto.[1] The second legend also explains the origin of that same little chapel. This is a story of Christ in the Big Bend, a story related not only to the chapel on El Cerrito de la Santa Cruz, but to the image of Christ in the church at Ojinaga, and in some respects to the origin of the church itself.

One day a long time ago—it is said—a stranger stopped and asked for a night's lodging at an adobe farmhouse in the long, green valley near the foot of El Cerrito de la Santa Cruz. The woman of the house gave him his supper and showed him to his room.

Next morning the stranger did not appear for breakfast. Having waited beyond her patience, the hostess finally opened the door a crack and peeked into the room.

To her astonishment, the smooth bed had not been slept in. To her further surprise, on the floor was a mysterious box, about the size of a coffin. With fear in her heart that was finally overcome by curiosity, she lifted the lid. With a great start she saw lying in the box a life-size image of Christ.

She fell to her knees and crossed herself; then quickly she arose, shut the box, threw her black mantilla over her head and dashed out of the house.

She ran as fast as she could along the sandy road into the village of Ojinaga. Breathlessly she entered the cool and shadowed church and did her obeisance before the altar; and soon she found the priest.

"Padre!" she exclaimed. "Only yesterday a man came to find lodging in my house. I gave him a bed for the night— today he is gone—instead there is a beautiful image of *Nuestro Padre Jesús* in a great box."

The priest marveled at the apparent miracle, put on his broad black hat, and went with the old woman as she retraced her steps through the sand to her valley farmhouse among the willows. The old lady showed the priest the room where the image lay. The priest crossed himself, held up his rosary cross for protection against black magic, and lifted the lid. He saw the image of Christ.

Turning to the old woman, he said, "Señora, this is a beautiful work of art. It is brought by a miracle from God for us to place in our poor church at Ojinaga. But it is much too fine a figure for our little run-down church. We must have a larger and finer church, one that is worthy of this miraculous image."

The priest went to the window and looked south across the cactus-ridden waste, at the sandy road that wound its way between the craggy, dry mountains of the Big Bend. He said:

"I must show this statue to the bishop in Chihuahua. I have been trying to get money for a new church but without success. Perhaps if I load this image on a wagon and drive it to Chihuahua, the bishop will be convinced. When he sees the wonderful beauty of the statue and hears my story of the miracle, I am sure that he will then give us money for a church suitable for this image."

Before the day was over, the priest was on his way with a mule hitched to his wagon, in which lay the image, secured with ropes. As he passed along the road around the base of the cliff where the devil's cave looked out upon the valley, he shuddered and crossed himself. When the wagon had passed halfway round the mountain, the mule—characteristically—stopped.

The Padre urged the mule on with the lines. The mule would not budge. Was it a spell of the devil?

"Mule!" he cried. "You are drawing a divine burden. Proceed! You are doing work of the Lord!"

Still the mule, baking under the hot sun, balked and refused to comply.

The Padre whipped the mule. But the wheels stood motionless in the sandy ruts. He yelled and whipped all at once; still the mule, though flinching, would not go.

As a last resort the priest drew up his black skirts, climbed down·from the wagon, and knelt in the sandy road. He began to pray that the mule be suffered to go on down the road to Chihuahua so that his little town might have a new church.

As he prayed the air began to stir. The wind lifted gusts of biting sand before it. Black clouds coursed the sky, shafts of lightning speared the ground, and rolling thunder rocked back and forth between the mountainous rocks and cliffs. Rain began to pock the sand, then came down in blinding torrents.

Rainwater pouring from his hat-brim, the priest concluded: "The image does not want to go to Chihuahua. It wants to stay here in the place for which it is intended. This image can never be taken from Ojinaga."

He climbed back into the wagon, reined the mule around and drove back through the downpour into Ojinaga. He took the image into the church, where it was erected in its proper place.

Next day, when the priest told the people of the valley what had occurred, they decided to do something special to commemorate the miracle. They built a little shrine on top of El Cerrito de la Santa Cruz as a memorial to the miraculous acquisition of the image.

The shrine has been put to constant use by worshipers since it was built. Once a year the shrine's cross is removed on Holy Cross Day and is taken by a procession down the mountain to the house where the image is reputed to have been found by the old woman. Valley farmers come to this house and pray for prosperity and rain, and in due time the cross is restored to its shrine on top of the mountain.

Another story dealing with the origin of the image is related to the devil's cave story, but not to the origin of the shrine.

When the story of how the devil was imprisoned is told, it

is sometimes followed by the story of a good and handsome man who appeared in the town of Ojinaga shortly afterward. He was loved by everybody for his helpful and friendly works in the village. He was a very strange young man, for he never grew old. The people came to accept this eternal youth of the kind stranger, who lived with them for a hundred years, giving to the poor in spirit.

One day he failed to appear in his accustomed haunts in the town. He was not in the plaza, nor in the church, nor at work in the fields. The anxious people searched everywhere for the kind stranger, but he was nowhere to be found. In the evening, as the church bells began to ring, the people turned from the search and filed along the narrow streets to worship. They entered the church, knelt before the altar, and raised their eyes to behold a miracle.

There behind the altar was a beautiful image of their kind, young stranger. There could be no mistake, he was the same. Marveling, they read at the foot of the image, *Nuestro Señor Jesús.*

Another story following the same lines tells of a beautiful lady who appeared in the town of Ojinaga, just after the disappearance of the miraculous young man. She also lived in the village a hundred years, helping the needy, winning the love of all, and never growing old. At the end of another century, she also disappeared. The people searched, and gave up only to answer the evening call to worship. There in the church stood a new image—the image of their kind lady—and the inscription at the foot read, *María, Madre de Dios.*

Two other stories about the origin of the image of Christ in the Ojinaga church are similar in general outline. It is said that in the days before Ojinaga had a church, an elderly man approached a group busily working their fields. He asked the people if they wanted to buy his statue, an image of Christ, for their proposed church. The people said they would like to see it before they made up their minds. The old man told them to meet him at a certain time and place and they would try to come to terms.

When the people arrived to discuss the matter, they found a beautiful image of Christ standing where they were to meet the stranger. They waited, but the stranger never appeared. The priest and the people decided that the image was somehow a miraculous gift from God, so they decided to build their church on that spot; and there it stands today.

The priest then—as in the other tale—thought it best to take the image to Chihuahua as evidence to convince the bishop that Ojinaga should have a fine church. The priest loaded the image on a mule, but the mule would not move. He decided the load was too heavy for the animal, so he placed the image in a wagon and started out. He had gone but a little way when the wagon wheels fell off the hubs, landing the wagon bed flat on the road. Everybody decided that the image did not want to go to Chihuahua. So the priest wrote a letter to the bishop, and he sent money for a fine church which was then built for the image.

The second variant tells a similar story, differing in some details. It is said that a long time ago the priest at Ojinaga decided his church desperately needed an image of Christ. As the church could not afford a fine, expensive image, the Padre decided to have a cheap one made of clay. He called in two artists to make the image. Without asking any questions, the artists apparently set to work, though they were never seen either modeling their image or going about in the town. It was rumored about that they did their work at night and slept all day.

At last the artists were through, and called the priest to see if the image was satisfactory. He observed that they had created a marvelous work of art. He told the men he would return the next day to pay them for their effort. But when he came back, the artists had mysteriously disappeared. They were never found, and they never received pay for their wonderful work.

But they left behind the beautiful image to comfort and inspire the worshipers in the twin towns of Presidio and Ojinaga.

A tradition arising from these tales about the image of Christ in the Ojinaga church is that God will not allow either the image or its vestments to be taken from the church or from the town. This tradition has its exception, however, in a story that is related in its details to the stories about the origin of the image.

The story goes that the people of Julimes, a village to the south, once wanted to borrow the figure of Christ to use with a special mass in their small church. Messengers came up from Julimes to ask the Padre of Ojinaga if they might be permitted to take the image to their town. The Padre agreed, and the figure was loaded carefully into a wagon. In charge of the two men, the journey to Julimes began.

They had gone but a few miles when a thunderstorm broke upon them. There was much lightning and thunder and the rain fell in sheets. Because of the storm, they were forced to turn back through the rain with the image to Ojinaga.

The next day being clear, the men from Julimes started out again in their wagon with its miraculous load. They had gone only a short distance when the load seemed to grow too heavy for the mules. The drivers urged the mules on, but they would not stir. The animals grew so tired that they lay down in the road with their harness tangled all about them in a hopeless mess.

One of the drivers jog-trotted back to Ojinaga to tell the priest what had happened. The priest came out with the man to the scene, so that he might judge the circumstances for himself. He looked at the load and the mules, then knelt upon the ground. He informed the image, "They are taking Thee there only for a short while and will bring Thee back safely."

No sooner had he pronounced these words than the mules were on their feet and on their way with the reconciled image to Julimes.

Another story has it that the forces of evil may not tamper with Ojinaga's miraculous likeness of Christ.

It is told that in 1914 Ojinaga was in the hands of revolutionists. Many were fighting out of patriotism, but a few of those who were fighting only for loot and adventure laughed at the superstitions about the image in Ojinaga's church. In defiance of God and man, these men went into the church one day, paying absolutely no respect to the house of God. They tore the robes from the image of Christ with the evil intention of taking them outside and showing them off in the streets as proof of their own sacrilege.

While these men were desecrating the church, they heard rifle-fire outside. The Federals were attacking the town. Hearing the shots, the bandits drew their pistols and ran out into the street. Each was killed as he came out of the building. The last man, who was carrying the cloak of Christ over his arm, was drilled by a bullet just before he made it to the door. He fell dead on the floor, tangled in the cloak, as grim proof that nothing pertaining to the image can be carried from the church.

The image stands today behind the altar in the Ojinaga church. It is considered by many to be a thing of miracles. It is said that the hair and fingernails of the image grow. In time of drought, the image goes out at night and walks the fields to bring rain. On mornings after a rain, the vestments of the image are said to be wet and muddy, and goathead stickers are found clinging to the robes.

There are obvious relationships and parallels in these stories. In the first place, they are duplicated in other towns and other churches in the Southwest. The Latin-American strongly localizes his legends. This Ojinaga-Presidio tale is linked to the story of the Devil's Grotto in that one version of it contains an alternate explanation of the shrine on top of El Cerrito de la Santa Cruz. Most of the stories have several details in common: (1) the image is miraculously bestowed upon the town by a stranger or strangers; (2) the image is used in an attempt to get either a church or a new church for the town; (3) an unsuccessful attempt is made to carry the image out of town; (4) the tradition that the image may not be taken from the town or even from the church is somehow strengthened.

It is perhaps worthy of note also that in the legends of Christ and the devil in the Big Bend, Christ is the deity of rain and productivity, while the devil is the evil power of drought and destruction. These traditions are parallel with Indian rain-god and drought-god traditions—as well as with legendary substance the world over—and indicate a probable uniting of Catholic tradition with aboriginal legends. It is interesting also that all these legends attribute power and personality to the image. When the story is told by the Mexican, he does not say it was God's will that the image remain in Ojinaga. Rather, he says, "The statue did not want to go to Chihuahua."

1. See "The Devil in the Big Bend," *Folk Travelers* (Publication of the Texas Folklore Society, No. XXV [Dallas, 1953], 205-16).

The Ghost of the Hutto Ranch

JOHN Q. ANDERSON

FOR MANY YEARS before the old house burned in the 1940's, tales of the Ghost of the Hutto Ranch were widely known in southeastern Wheeler County in the Panhandle of Texas. Though details varied with the imagination of the teller, these tales always followed the same general pattern: when the occupant of the ranch house expected visitors, especially at night, the thump of boot heels on the broad front veranda would be heard; the steps would advance to the front door and the doorknob would rattle. But when the door was opened, no one was there—nothing but the silence of the prairie night. Later on, the same sound of boot heels on the porch would again be heard. Again the doorknob would rattle. A few seconds afterward, the measured tread of heavy boots would be heard ascending the stairs to the second story. Investigation would reveal the presence of no living body, either on the veranda or on the stairs.

As tenants of the old house came and went over the years, the mysterious activities of the Ghost of the Hutto increased. Some people reported that the boot heels were always heard when company was expected, any time of the year—even in broad daylight; others maintained that the Ghost came only during the full moon of October; some were quite certain that the date was October 12. All these people connected the Ghost with an obvious bullet hole in the wall of the house and with a dark stain, said to be that of human blood, in the northeast room.

Since I lived for a number of years as a boy in the neighborhood of the Hutto Ranch, I heard the tales of the Ghost of the Hutto many times. Later on, I learned all I could about the history of the ranch, some of which was indeed dramatic enough to give rise to ghost stories.

Records indicate that the acreage first belonged to Jack Wright. In the 1880's, R. B. Masterson, a successful rancher in Travis County, bought out Wright and ran his Long S brand over much of southeastern Wheeler County. Masterson sold the range to Robinson and Sauls, who, in turn, sold it to A. B. Hutto in 1898.[1] From then on the area was known as the Hutto Ranch. Hutto sold off part of his range to farmers after 1900, but retained the house and about five thousand acres of land. In 1924 Hutto sold these holdings to Ed and Champ Davis, who with the range they had bought from Masterson in 1892 came to own forty-two sections of land in Wheeler County and in Beckham County, Oklahoma.[2] During my boyhood the Hutto Ranch was part of the Davis Figure 2 Ranch.

Although the construction date of the Hutto Ranch house is not known, it was probably built after Wheeler County was organized as the first county in the Panhandle in 1879. Since there were no railroads in the Panhandle at that time, lumber for the house was freighted in by wagon, from either Dodge City, Sherman, or Fort Reno, Indian Territory. The house had four large square rooms and a kitchen on the ground floor, a large upstairs and attic, and wide verandas on the south and east. Painted a dark gray, the house was set in a large yard filled with elm, mulberry, and cottonwood trees, and enclosed in a stout wire-mesh fence. Surrounded by a wide plain of buffalo grass, the house was a landmark on the rolling prairie. Since most of the dwellings in the Panhandle in the early days were sod houses or two-room shanties, the Hutto house was indeed luxurious.

At a distance from the house, on the edge of Dry Creek, were the corrals, sheds, and barns. The walls of these buildings were of a gray stone which, like the lumber for the house, had been hauled in; the plains provided no such rock. The sturdy structure of the Hutto headquarters indicated that the ranch had been planned as the permanent home of its builder, no fly-by-night rancher who expected to get rich quick from grazing a herd on state land and then to move on to a more settled part of the country. Only a mile from the present Texas-Oklahoma line, the Hutto was on a short cut on the military road leading from Fort Sill, Indian Territory, to Old Mobeetie and Fort Elliott, Texas. The deep ruts of the road, though covered over with mesquite grass, were still visible a few years ago. Not more than four miles from the Hutto was a sand-blow sheltered by a hill which apparently had been a favorite camping place of Kiowas and Comanches. As a boy, I picked up many arrowheads and Indian-head pennies at the place. Thus, the Hutto was an outpost of civilization when the ranch house was first built, a fact that makes its pretentiousness all the more remarkable.

As might be expected, the Hutto Ranch ghost stories involve murder—three murders, in fact. Characteristically, names and dates are missing.

The first murder at the Hutto occurred during a dance that was being held at the ranch house. People had come long distances from other ranches and from nesters' dugouts and sod shanties for the festive occasion. The furniture had been removed from the northeast room where the dancing was going on. A young cowboy was sitting calmly on his haunches against the wall watching the dancers when another cowhand walked in the door, drew his six-shooter, and shot the first one dead. The dying man fell forward on the floor and his lifeblood flowed out on the pine flooring. The murderer's motive remains unknown. In fact, no more of the story is told, although people who later lived in the house maintained that no amount of scrubbing would remove the black stain of that cowboy's blood from the floor. The large, irregular blot was there to be seen until the house was destroyed by fire.

The story of the second murder at the Hutto contains more details, though names and dates are again missing. According to the tale, in the early days a young rancher established his headquarters at the Hutto, stocked the range, and hired hands. He also brought his young wife to live at the ranch. Women were so scarce in the Panhandle at the time that cowboys reportedly rode for miles just to get a glimpse of one. Apparently the young rancher's wife justified such interest, for she was exceptionally beautiful. The interest of one of the hired hands exceeded mere curiosity; he fell madly in love with the boss's wife. The rancher soon became aware of the situation, paid the cowboy off, and told him to take his plunder and leave.

Although the cowboy showed a great deal of resentment at the time, he did leave the ranch. He soon returned, however, fired with liquor. Not wanting trouble, the rancher asked his foreman to talk the drunken cowboy into leaving quietly. The cowboy refused. He openly threatened the rancher and eventually accosted him in the yard. The rancher tried to reason with his former hand. Emboldened by whiskey, the cowboy began to curse the rancher, who, to avoid a fight, turned and went into the house. The cowboy stamped through a puddle of mud, walked into the house, and climbed up into the middle of the bed with his muddy boots on. The angry rancher pulled out his gun and ordered the cowboy out of the house. Sober enough to understand that command, the cowboy went outside, swearing that he would "get even." The rancher followed him through the yard to the barn. There the cowboy attempted to draw his gun, and the rancher shot him. The cowboy fell against the rock wall of the barn and his lifeblood spattered on the white stone. The dark stain was visible long afterward.

There had been no witness to the killing, but to make certain that justice was done the rancher dispatched a rider forty miles to Mobeetie for a coroner. The body of the cowboy, covered with a tarp to keep off the drizzling rain, lay during the night where he had fallen. Past this point, the story does not go. Nor is there any indication of where the cowboy was buried, though a likely spot would be in the grove of mulberry trees that stand near the site of the house.

The circumstance of the third murder is not known, though tale-tellers were always careful to specify three. Since neither of the other tales mentions the bullet hole in the wall of the house, perhaps the third killing was somehow connected with it. Either of the first two murders would, of course, be sufficient basis for the tale of the Ghost of the Hutto; therefore the third may be no more than an addition to obtain the magical number three.

The manner of appearance of the Ghost of the Hutto is unique only in that the sound of boot heels was always emphasized by tellers of the tale, thus relating the story definitely to the early history of the house. Vance Randolph in *Ozark Superstitions* records similar activities of a ghost in Missouri:

An old lady in McDonald County, Missouri, told me that she once sat alone in her two-room cabin, with the door bolted and the window fastened on the inside. Suddenly she heard the latch on the door move, and the sound of a heavy man walking across the floor. "I could hear one of his boots squeak at every step."[3]

He also reports a similar incident at Zinc, Arkansas, in which a couple tried to sleep in a haunted house. The barred door burst open, but no one was there.[4] Records indicate a number of haunted ranch houses in Texas[5] as well as several instances of return of the dead for various reasons.[6]

The most obvious motif in the tales of the Ghost of the Hutto is that of the unlaid ghost, a common theme in literature and folklore. The dead return to complete unfinished business, to warn or inform, to punish or protect, or to impart information. Especially are the ghosts of those persons who died by violence

—murder, suicide, or accident—likely to come back. Often such returned dead seek a living person, closely related, to perform some act which will release the ghost from earth. Even if the Ghost of the Hutto originally returned for revenge—the most likely reasons for both the first and second murders committed at the house—that motivation was lost from the story. In its place, a "logical" reason had to be invented; consequently the Ghost returned, it was said, to protect some treasure hidden upstairs. With other boys, I searched the upstairs and attic of the house without finding any such treasure. That fact did not discourage the repetition of the treasure theme of the tale, however.

A second significant motif is that the ghost most frequently returned during the full of the moon. This theme ties the tale in with the numerous superstitions connected with the moon. But exactly why some versions specified the full moon in October or the specific date of October 12, I was never able to ascertain.

Although the bloodstains on the floor of the house and on the rock wall of the barn were always mentioned in stories of the murders at the Hutto, they were strangely never mentioned in connection with the ghost.[7] Even so, the presence of the stains contributed to the mystery of the house and doubtless assisted in the development of the ghost story.

Most citizens of the community put little stock in the Ghost of the Hutto. Some explained away the sound of the boot heels on the veranda, the rattling of the doorknob, and the footsteps on the stairs as the scraping of tree limbs on the roof, as the shifting and settling of the house at night, as the scampering of mice and rats, or even as a peculiar geological formation underneath the house which expanded during the day, contracted at night, and permitted the house to creak and groan. Such explanations did nothing, however, to discourage repetition of the tale.

The tale illustrates the same desire for explanation of the

unknown that led to creation myths and "why" stories. Given an unusual, old house, the known history of which involved murder and violence, the strangeness was inevitably captured in a tale of mystery. Though such a tale might be told by a skeptic to listeners who doubted, the very telling of the tale made it part of the oral lore of the area, as indeed was the Ghost of the Hutto Ranch.

1. Millie Jones Porter, *Memory Cups of Panhandle Pioneers* (Clarendon, Texas, 1945), p. 142.

2. *Ibid.*, p. 196. Although Mrs. Porter states that Champ Davis told her that the ranch was purchased in 1901, my father, A. S. Anderson, who knew Champ Davis intimately from 1918 until 1941, says that the date was 1892, which is evidently correct since Ed Davis died in 1900 and was alive when the brothers bought the ranch.

3. Vance Randolph, "Ghost Stories," *Ozark Superstitions* (New York, 1947), p. 215.

4. *Ibid.*, p. 216.

5. *Publications of the Texas Folklore Society* contain these: Frank Goodwyn, "Folk-Lore of the King Ranch Mexicans," *Southwestern Lore,* IX (1931), 48-62; Fannie E. Ratchford, "Legend Making on the Concho," *Coyote Wisdom,* XIV (1938), 178; and Soledad Pérez, "The German Girl," *The Healer of Los Olmos,* XXIV (1951), 95-96.

6. *Ibid.* C. L. Sonnichsen, "Mexican Spooks from El Paso," *Straight Texas,* XIII (1937), 120-29; Julia Beazley, "The Black Cat of Cole's Plantation," *Straight Texas,* XIII (1937), 182-84; "The Restless Bridegroom," *Backwoods to Border,* XVIII (1943), 141-42.

7. Dr. C. C. Doak, head of the Department of Biology, Texas A. and M. College, assures me that the stains I saw years after the murder were quite likely made by human blood. Such stains are almost permanent and are especially likely to remain in porous wood. In fact, the stain of human blood is almost impossible to remove.

Spanish Folklore from South Texas

ALFREDO R. GARCIA

Mal de Ojo

UNTIL a few years ago, the people of Spanish descent who lived in the Rio Grande Valley believed in *mal de ojo*. Now *mal de ojo*, the evil eye, is not black magic, but rather the power with which Nature endows some people whereby they can cause others to become sick. This power, located in the eyes, is in some cases so strong that it produces an electrical discharge which will shatter breakable objects, such as glassware. The spell is not cast purposely; it results, rather, from the failure of a "powerful" individual to satisfy his urge to touch a person he likes, or some feature of that person, with his hands at the time the urge appears.

Most *mal de ojo* happens among children, especially babies —who, being pretty, naturally attract more eyes and, consequently, suffer more attacks of the evil eye. But do not think that grown-ups are not susceptible to this malady. I can well remember when in the late 1920's a certain Señor Rufino Alcantar, now deceased (*Que en paz descanse*, may his soul rest in peace), was a victim of *mal de ojo*. Señor Alcantar was a short, fat, baldheaded, ugly man. He had a wife who was not as fat and not as beautiful as he, and she had borne him five children. Señor Alcantar was a butcher in a modern meat market, and though not a man of letters, earned a nice living wage for his family.

Behind the counter in his butcher shop, Señor Alcantar

was always immaculately dressed in clean white apron, white shirt, and white cap as he politely waited on his customers. He had built up a good clientele consisting of the high class women of Raymondville. Women shoppers as a rule are astute meat buyers. They have found out that a casual compliment to the butcher gets them a few more ounces of meat.

Señor Alcantar had worked for several years and daily was subject to many complimentary remarks about his person. Certainly his wife shared in this knowledge and all were a happy bunch.

One day Cuca, his little girl, came to my house and asked my mother to lend her mother two eggs because her father was sick, very sick of *mal de ojo,* and the eggs were needed in the process of curing him. Señora Alcantar took the eggs and broke them into a small saucer. She placed them under the bed toward the man's head and then with a lighted cigarette she made a series of smoke crosses over the man's body. She offered a few *rezos* (prayers) and occasionally tapped the ashes from her cigarette into the palm of her hand and made a little cross on the head and chest of Señor Alcantar, who was clad in B.V.D.'s; pajamas were not in fashion at that time. The Señora then covered him with a sheet and gave him a hot drink of *te de canela* (cinnamon tea).

The next day Señor Alcantar's malady of severe headache and shoulder pains had disappeared, and he was up and ready to resume his duties. The eggs underneath his bed had turned to a whitish color; in the center and over the yolk was a little circle in the shape of an eye. This was ample proof that one of his lady customers had had the urge to touch him, and thus had cast *mal de ojo* upon him. Had he known which one of the ladies was involved, the cure would have been simplified; he could merely have called the evil-doer and had her touch him. That would have cured him just as effectively as the eggs under the bed.

La Rifera

DON EDUARDO CANTU was an old Spanish settler in the Rio Grande Valley. His parents were originally from Spain and had settled in Old Mexico; later he had himself moved across the river into what is now Willacy County, Texas, in the northern part of the Valley. Through hard work and systematic saving, he had become a large land owner. After he had outlived three wives who collectively brought him eighteen children, he died, and his estate was divided among his heirs. None of the children had had a formal education but all had been reared in the best environment that a good Catholic home could provide.

While the majority of the heirs prospered with the land they inherited, the black sheep of the family, Nicolas, did not do so well. He was a hard worker, but it seems his ranching ability was below par. One hardship after another nibbled at his possessions; he became desperate and did not know exactly what to do. It hurt his pride that he could not get ahead of or at least keep on the level of his brothers. He prayed, he worked, and he hoped—yet the powers seemed against him.

He faced a dilemma. Should he sell his ranch and move into town with his large family, or should he remain at the ranch and keep struggling? At that time in the city there lived one Doña María, *la rifera* (the fortune teller). Doña María was known far and wide to be great and exact in the secret art of foretelling the future with her deck of *barajas* (playing cards). She would take any person into her private home and for a small fee gaze into the future and in a few minutes tell the person with a measure of certainty the chances of failure or success in any enterprise.

Nicolas decided to pay a visit to Doña María. His wife, particularly, urged him to go see *la rifera,* for she knew Doña María had told the fortune to Don Plutarco Pérez who had been so lucky as to have oil discovered on his land. "Anda que

te heche la rifa Doña María," she said. "A ver que nos manda
Dios." ("Go and let Doña María tell you the future. Let's see
what God will send us.")

Nicolas cranked his Model T and in a few minutes was
headed for the city to consult with Doña María. The roads
were dusty and rough, for there were no farm-to-market roads
in existence then. His Model T was a good-running little car
and in good condition because he was the only one in the
family who could drive it. Being under the arbor most of the
time, the Model T kept a nice gloss, and its red-and-white
tires gave it added personality. The trip was uneventful and
he arrived at Doña María's house, which was in the *Mejiquito*
(little Mexico) part of town.

Five other persons were in the waiting room waiting their
turn for an interview. How lucky he was, only five clients
ahead! Nicolas came in, took his hat off, and sat down to wait.
The room's furniture consisted merely of two benches along
one side, two wooden boxes, and, at the end of the room, a torn
canvas cot. The walls were barren except for a picture of St.
Christopher. There were no drapes.

In less than two hours Nicolas was in a private room relating his problems and his wishes to Doña María. She sat on her
bed and spread her cards—a deck of Spanish cards, which she
handled with great dexterity—on a low table in front of her.
The table was shrouded in black cloth. In the corner of the
room were a number of burning candles. Little pictures of the
Virgin Mary and a few saints' images decorated the walls. The
room was heavy with incense. Doña María's dress was not
extraordinary, though she did wear a number of odd-looking
rings on her fingers. Her hair was braided and her tresses hung
over her shoulders and over her breast.

For fifty cents Doña María told a good fortune. She would
place the cards on the table first in one pattern, then in another,
and then in another. All the time while she was changing the
cards she would be explaining the meaning of each card; then

she would double-check by repeating the process. She spoke in a sort of a chant, at the end relating each card to the others and showing their relation to the client.

At the conclusion of her *rifa*, Doña María told Nicolas that the stars indicated he was to possess money. But Nicolas had asked whether or not he should sell his land, and he insisted on a definite answer to this question. She then told him the cards indicated that if he sold the land he would get some money, but if he didn't sell his land he would own more.

Nicolas paid his fee and returned to his *rancho*. He talked it over with his wife and decided that maybe they could sell part of the land and keep part. So they sold some of the land very cheaply and moved into town.

A few years passed while Nicolas made a living working where he could in town. Then the depression was over, the war broke out, and things began to change. By this time irrigation canals had been put in near the land that Nicolas still owned, and the war demanded production of all sorts of vegetables. Nicolas rented out his little house in the city and went back to his farm. He planted fifty acres in cabbages and had a good crop, which he sold for as much as $110 a ton. He cleared more than $10,000 that year. He could not help but believe that Doña María had predicted correctly. No oil was discovered on his land but the "cabbage" kept rolling in, thanks to *la rifera*, Doña María.

Home Remedies for Arthritis

WALTER TAYLOR

"No one dies of arthritis, but, oh, how they sometimes wish they would." The woman who wrote that must have been writing from the depths of personal experience with this disease which, with its cousins—rheumatism, rheumatic fever, and gout—today claims more than 7,500,000 victims in the United States.

The earliest history of arthritis is found recorded in the bones of dinosaurs which lived two hundred million years before man. Fossils of the Java Ape Man and the Neanderthal Man, as well as early Egyptian mummies, all display the tell-tale signs of crusted outgrowth which the disease leaves.

From earliest time man has sought to relieve the pain of his swollen joints and remove the cause before bony growth destroys their usefulness entirely. An extant Babylonian prescription reads: "The king should be anointed while he rests. ... He should have incantations performed over pure water, in the basin in which he regularly washes. ... Quickly the arthritis will leave...." Nicholas Culpeper's *Complete Herbal* records twenty-one English herbs which were reputed to be "virtuous" for allaying pain from "the hard humours of knots in the joints." A poltice of the juice of cuckow-point mixed with hot ox dung may be helpful, this once-ubiquitous volume reports.

Modern medical remedies have been strange and varied. Artificially induced and controlled fevers ease pain sometimes.

The venom of bees and snakes has been injected directly into the affected joints. The extraction of teeth, tonsils, and, indeed, the removal of anything removable from the body have been attempted in the effort to excise the disease's cause.

After all this, exercise and heat, together with sufficient rest and proper diet, still form the backbone of most successful treatment today. As one writer says, ". . . We even today have few effective treatments, and it is no wonder that the Babylonians combatted [the disease] with incantations."

In an effort to collect a few of the folk prescriptions in circulation today, the following letter was addressed to the Letters columns of the Fort Worth *Star-Telegram* and three other southern newspapers:

SIR:
    I am a college student who has arthritis. I am interested in making a collection of all the old and new home remedies for the disease. Perhaps your readers can help me.

From all over Texas as well as from other parts of the South came postal cards and letters. Some were written on fine, embossed stationery in practiced calligraphy; others were inscribed with pencil on simple, lined tablet-paper in irregular Palmer script. One from Fort Worth was almost illegibly misspelled on a scrap of brown wrapping paper; another from Teague, Texas, was scrabbled by the unsteady hand of an eighty-six-year-old.

They offered sincere sympathy and advice and frequently promised daily prayer. Perhaps the sincerity adds to the authenticity of these strange medications as genuine folklore. To them I have added some "cures" suggested by my doctor and by a Negro maid. All are as current as this month's issue of a medical journal.

The strangest remedials are those which purport to cure by some odylic power inherent in an amulet. Only seven of these phylacteries have been reported, but most of them have been suggested several times, which shows they are widely known.

Copper has long been worn to cure arthritis. Bracelets, anklets, necklaces, and rings made of this metal all have done wonderful things for sufferers. A bracelet of copper has "helped more than anything I have tried," reports "A Friend" in Fort Worth. A lady in Matador, Texas, wears two such bracelets which she is "afraid to pull off for fear the pains will come back." She adds that a friend of hers "spent his farm and all the money he had before he heard about putting brass on his wrists and ankles. Inside of a year he was out of his wheelchair going where he pleased."

One informant tells of seeing a little girl, a victim of arthritis, whose fingers were stained green from the wearing of many copper rings. A strand of copper wire makes a crude ring or bracelet. An iron finger ring with a copper "setting" seems to be a remedy found only in the Southwest.

I was also told by a correspondent to go into a dark room and rub the joints with a copper penny for relief.

Another metal with curative powers is zinc. Some people have put zinc plates in their shoes for healing.

Three writers suggest putting a little powdered sulphur in each shoe. "Do this consistently for several months," said one lady, while another prescribed, more elaborately, that the sulphur be replaced each day and the rite be practiced only in alternate weeks. Another letter, entirely punctuated with erratically placed colons, suggested the sulphur cure even though the writer, a woman, had never tried it herself. "A gentleman sent me the remedy who said it cured him," she adds by way of recommendation, "and he is a very thoughtful man."

Many people have carried a buckeye or a horse chestnut to cure their pain. A former actor, an Oklahoma citizen whose printed letterhead boasted the fact that he held a Master of Arts degree, told a strange but true tale of being given a chestnut by a stagehand many years ago. A leg pain which had prevented the writer from finishing a dance on stage that night was immediately relieved and did not return until a day three weeks later when, in a moment of skepticism, he threw the chestnut out of the window of a train car. "That night my leg was so sore I could not go on with the act," he avows.

My doctor testifies that a raw Irish potato carried in the left hip pocket is relied upon by some arthritics. I have heard that potato peelings are also used, but I do not know how.

Job's-tears, the Asiatic grass seeds, are sometimes strung as beads and worn around the neck as an ornament and as a phylactery.

A Negro maid supplied this bit of witchery. A piece of twine in which nine knots have been tied and which has been soaked in kerosene should be worn nine days for aid.

Unusual too are the many ointments with which people rub themselves or which they apply to their affected joints in an effort to ease the pain which accompanies every motion.

The elderly writer in Teague, Texas, recounted her experience with liniment which she intentionally used to blister her joints. "In two weeks the pain was gone. The blister was gone. It's been well ever since." Of course this treatment would have to be practiced judiciously when *all* of the joints are affected.

The note written on wrapping paper by a Fort Worth citizen said that she put a cupful of Epsom salts in a hot tub of water and soaked herself in this for half an hour. "The bath water was real yellow when I got out," she says. "Guess it was poison and presperation [sic] from my body."

Almost a catholican is the omnipotent oil of the peanut. Taken internally it is reputed to aid in many diseases. Used as a rubbing lubricant, it is said to impart great relief to rheumatic sufferers. Snake oil, available at the drugstore, is also recommended.

One writer keeps a bottle of castor oil and turpentine, mixed in equal portions, by her bedside for frequent use as a lotion. Another applies a mixture of salt and white gasoline to the inflamed areas. Needless to say, greater difficulty might be avoided if the patient abstains from smoking while undergoing this and the preceding treatments.

From North Carolina comes the suggestion that warm vinegar makes a soothing application. The famous vinegar-and-brown-paper cure which has long been used as a specific for headaches and which is immortalized in the rhyme about Jack and Jill also came to me from North Carolina, this time as a palliative for rheumatic pains.

One other out-of-state remedy is worth quoting in full. To the Atlanta *Journal and Constitution* magazine section for January 4, 1953, a reader wrote: "Another good remedy I have is half molasses and half creosote. I paint the affected joints with it, let it stay on about half an hour and then take it off with kerosene."

Taken internally are numerous draughts, pills, and ptisans prescribed by folk for the relief of arthritis. Some of them involve the infusion of herbs and roots in whiskey. A physician, telling of a Presbyterian elder who ascribed his cure to such an elixir, suggests that "possibly the corn whiskey was most beneficial because it picked up his appetite when he had none."

Evidently the currently most popular cure is a tea brewed from untreated seed of alfalfa. Everyone who has arthritis seems to have tried, to be trying, or to be intending to try it, and each has a different formula for its preparation. From Murphy, North Carolina, from Del Rio, Texas, and from points between came various recipes and dosages. Basically the recipe calls for boiling a quarter of a cup of alfalfa seed in a quart of water for twenty minutes in an enamel pan. (An aluminum pan will be stained.) A glass of the strained "tea" is then drunk several times a day.

Letters telling of the effect produced by this alfalfa seed tea read like testimonials for the philosopher's stone itself. "In a year you will be so much better that you will want to keep this up for the rest of your life," writes a Texas correspondent.

Another victim says, "I'm good as new. I had spent lots of money on doctors and cured myself for 65c." They say, "My neighbor's aunt was helpless in a wheelchair. . . . Now she is working in a grocery store," or, "My wife used to have to dress me; now I'm back at work." So the word echoes across the land, and people rush to try the new cure. As one writer added, "It can't do you no harm to try it."

Much touted is a concoction of fruit juices mixed with a little Epsom salts and cream of tartar. This recipe is found in all parts of the South, but it, too, varies slightly from place to place. In the variations we see one example of folklore's "alteration through transmission." When the formula first came to my attention fifteen years ago, one of the ingredients was the juice of the grapefruit. Though two correspondents still use grapefruit, two others substitute grape juice. Evidently it is one or several of the *other* constituents which produce the healing.

Basically this potion is made from the juice of three grapefruit, three oranges, and three lemons. The peelings from these fruits are decocted, and the strained decoction is added to the juices. One tablespoonful of Epsom salts and one teaspoonful of cream of tartar are added too. This mixture is to be taken at the rate of two ounces a day.

The remedy with the longest history calls for taking pokeberry juice in some form. A simple version calls for taking one ripe berry a day for nine days, stopping nine days, and then taking nine more. This is continued until twenty-seven berries have been taken. The Walnut Springs, Texas, writer who recommended this reports that his neighbor "declares she takes nine a day," but adds, "I think she got the directions mixed."

A friend in South Carolina told of finding a postal card written in 1898 by a woman who later studied medicine and is now retired. My friend wondered if the now-retired physician would still tell her patients to "Put a good handful of dried pokeberries into a quart of whiskey and let it stand a day or two. Take one teaspoonful 3 times a day."

Noah Webster defines the pokeweed as a bacciferous American herb whose root is poisonous. Nevertheless, a Tennessee informant suggests: "Put as many slivers of poke root as can be held between the middle finger and thumb of the left hand and cut on each side of the hand. Cut these pieces in half and put in a quart of whiskey and let stand seven days. Take a tablespoonful three times a day for seven days. Rest a few days and repeat." The rest is probably necessary.

One ounce of dandelion root boiled for twenty minutes in one and a half pints of water was recommended by only one writer, a North Carolinian. This makes a tea similar to the alfalfa tea.

Soak a white egg overnight in the juice of four lemons and in the morning drink the lemon juice, urges a Dallas man in a letter written on interoffice memo sheets. The eggshell, which must be white, will be soft after its immersion because the lemon juice dissolves out the calcium, he tells me.

A cure using oil of wintergreen came first from Fort Worth. It calls for taking orally one drop of the oil in a little sugar. On the second day two drops are taken. The amount is increased to nine drops at the rate of one more drop each day and then is brought slowly back down to one drop, after which the treatment is omitted for a week. A variation from Tennessee calls for a top limit of fifteen drops of wintergreen a day. Following this routine enabled a housewife to "lay down on the floor and kick my heels up as high as any young person," she attests with justifiable pride.

The ancient sulphur and molasses tonic comes now in a new form as an electuary for arthritis. One half of a teaspoonful of sulphur may be mixed with a teaspoonful of honey and taken by mouth.

There remains but to mention two other letters in the internal medicine category. One recommended an extended use of a laxative. A postal card said in full: "A big dose of saltz [sic] once or twice each week for a year will wash it all out." The card was signed, simply and appropriately, "A Sympathizer."

It would be impossible to quote or paraphrase all of the regimens of diet and exercise submitted. The people who offered these were surest that theirs was the answer to the arthritic's problems. "I have the cure for you," said one. Another said graciously, "I aim to let your diet be . . ." A Floridian suggested that I "sojourn to" a particular San Antonio "school of health." She enclosed an article which she had written and which attributes America's high crime and illness rate to the over-fertilizing, bleaching, pasteurizing, fermenting, and spraying of our foods.

One writer says, "Drink all the milk you can hold." In contrast to this, in typical folk fashion, is the letter which says to take "no dairy products."

Goat's milk, raw vegetables, fruits, juices, and eggs are recommended. Starches and fats are not.

Baths of all kinds were named. Natural springs seem to have benefited many. None had been permanently cured by baths, however.

Many of these writers were unlearned folk who offered to share their good fortune with "a college student who has arthritis." Some were obviously cultured men and women. How is it that the folk pharmacopoeia in this one field is contributed to by all strata of society?

One reason for this phenomenon is that arthritis is closely tied in with the whole mental-emotional outlook of the victim, so that if he really believes that a particular remedy will help him, it may do so.

Another fact is made obvious by this collection. What helps one person may not help another. It is estimated that there are over fifty different kinds of arthritis, so despite the real relief brought to many, including myself, by cortisone and other hormones, the search for a cure must go on.

Yes, as the pain in millions of arthritic joints continues, the quest for relief continues too. Men and women, fellow-sufferers in all areas of the world, will share their discoveries with others until a real cure is found. Until that day folk everywhere will reply to scoffers as did the creosoted Georgian mentioned earlier: "You may think I am silly taking these remedies, but if you have arthritis, brother, you'll try anything!"

Contributors

RILEY AIKEN's fine collection published in *Puro Mexicano* (1935) under the title of "A Pack Load of Mexican Tales" is not likely to be forgotten. He is now back with more of the same. Mr. Aiken grew up on the Texas-Mexican border and has traveled extensively in Mexico in search of tales. He teaches modern languages in the Kansas State College at Emporia.

JOHN Q. ANDERSON, student of the Southwest, author of many articles, and editor of an important Civil War diary, spent his boyhood in the Texas Panhandle. He now teaches English at A. & M. College.

ROY BEDICHEK, for many years director of the Texas Interscholastic League, is an internationally known naturalist. His books include *Adventures with a Texas Naturalist* (1947), *Karánkaway Country* (1950), and *Educational Competition* (1955).

MODY C. BOATRIGHT is secretary and editor for the Texas Folklore Society. At the University of Texas he conducts a seminar in the literature of the Southwest. *Folk Laughter on the American Frontier* (1949) is one of his books.

During his twenty years of editorship J. FRANK DOBIE saw the Texas Folklore Society firmly established and its publications take an honored place in the literature of folklore. Besides the publications he has edited he has written a dozen or so books, all well known to members of the Society—*Tales of Old-Time Texas* (1955) being the latest.

ALFREDO GARCIA is a student at North Texas State College. He wrote his "Spanish Folklore from South Texas" while a member of George D. Hendricks' course in the life and literature of the Southwest.

JOSEPH W. HENDREN teaches English at Western Maryland College. In 1938 he published *A Study of Ballad Rhythm* and since that date he has continued to make notable contributions to ballad scholarship.

WILSON M. HUDSON, on the English faculty at the University of Texas, is associate editor of the publications of the Society. He has lived on the Border and in Mexico. His latest book is a collection of Andy Adams' campfire tales, *Why the Chisholm Trail Forks* (1956).

NORMAN (BROWNIE) MCNEIL will be remembered as the author of "Corridos of the Mexican Border" in *Mexican Border Ballads and Other Lore*, Texas Folklore Society Publication XXI. While a student at the University of Texas, McNeil was awarded the E. D. Farmer Scholarship for International Study. He went to Mexico, where he devoted most of his time to balladry. He later moved on to the ballad in English and wrote a dissertation on Child Ballads in the American Midwest, from which his present contribution is drawn. He now teaches at the Texas College of Arts and Industries at Kingsville.

ELTON MILES teaches English at the Sul Ross State College and collects folklore in the Big Bend. He has just edited the memoirs of Will Tom Carpenter, a Texas cattleman, for the University of Texas Press.

AMÉRICO PAREDES grew up in Brownsville, where he once worked on a Spanish language newspaper. He has received three degrees from the University of Texas, where his doctoral dissertation was on Gregorio Cortez, noted ballad hero and subject of his contribution to this volume. He is now teaching English at Texas Western College.

For many years preceding his recent death VICTOR SMITH lived in Alpine on what used to be called the Kansas City, Mexico and Orient Railroad. A teacher and architect by profession, he pursued folklore and archeology as an avocation. Among his noted contributions to the publications of the Society was "The Human Hand in Primitive Art."

R. C. STEPHENSON teaches comparative literature and Spanish at the University of Texas. His courses include one each in the ballad and the folktale. His knowledge of languages gives him a very wide range.

WALTER TAYLOR, as a member of John Lee Brooks' course in folklore at Southern Methodist University, was the winner of the Society's student contest in 1956 with the paper printed herein, "Home Remedies for Arthritis." He now teaches at Belhaven College, Jackson, Mississippi.

STITH THOMPSON was the editor of the first volume of the publications of the Society, *Round the Levee* (1916). From the University of Texas he moved on, eventually settling at Indiana, where he became dean of the graduate school and an internationally noted folklorist. His monumental *Motif-Index of Folk-Literature* is now appearing in a revised and enlarged edition. In the spring of 1956 he was visiting professor at the University of Texas.